THE OAKWOOD PRESS

CH00408484

FIFTY YEARS OF NEWPORT
1900-1949

Some Incidents in the History of Newport

and other events in Britain and the rest of the world during the same period

by
Cliff V. Knight
&
Alan V. Jones

THE OAKWOOD PRESS

© Oakwood Press & Cliff V. Knight & Alan V. Jones 2008

British Library Cataloguing in Publication Data
A Record for this book is available from the British Library
ISBN 978 0 85361 682 5

Typeset by Oakwood Graphics.
Printed by Cambrian Printers, Aberystwyth, Ceredigion.

Cliff Knight – 'A soldier for the Lord and a man of his people'

Few local people on their death have warranted and been acclaimed by a double-page spread in the South Wales Argus and whose funeral was attended by the Lord Mayor of Newport. This was in recognition of the life of Cliff Knight, a humble Christian whose faith was appreciated by the people he worked with in his job and for his devoted service as a Christian leader in Emmanuel Evangelical Church, Newport.

He gained popularity as a historian in Newport when he wrote four (with this book now five) books about Newport between the 1800s and 1950, mainly about the area of Pill in Newport. You may have read some of the books which Cliff researched and wrote.

At almost 90 his memory and mental agility was most remarkable. Each month he wrote a short article of interest and encouragement in the Church magazine and also contributed many items to the local newspapers. He continued to write these even from his bed up until a week or so before his death.

At his funeral there were people who remembered his devoted service in Pill and Newport during the period of redevelopment. It was a joy to get the draft of this book to the publishers a week or so before he died. He has left enough material for further books.

Front cover: Newport at dawn, a view in silhouette of the iconic Transport Bridge. The bridge opened in 1906 and it continues to dominate Newport's skyline to this day.

Tom Dart

Published by The Oakwood Press (Usk), P.O. Box 13, Usk, Mon., NP15 1YS.
E-mail: sales@oakwoodpress.co.uk
Website: www.oakwoodpress.co.uk

Contents

Cliff Knight with Newport's Transporter bridge in the background.

Foreword

by Mike Buckingham

It wasn't all that long after I came to Newport and met Cliff Knight for the first time I realised that as well as kindliness behind those twinkling eyes was a wealth of local knowledge.

Many, many times over the last 20 or so years I have quarried this rich source of information in my job as a journalist only to find that the small nuggets I have taken have caused not the least depletion. Cliff's knowledge is somehow capable of being constantly renewed and refined, a miraculous circumstance only partly explained by his scrupulous archival practices and encyclopaedic knowledge.

The central explanation, I suspect, is much more to do with miracles as the word is generally understood.

Cliff is a man of great Faith in God and therefore in man. He writes of the people of Newport because he has known and loved them for the largest part of a century.

When such compassion is linked with a desire to serve and record the people of this city thereby dignified, may we not call it a miracle of a small kind?

Newport and other parts of Gwent are generally well served by local historians. From our northernmost reaches in march and moor down to bustling, 21st century Newport, people are putting together the record of our journey through time. Amongst this diligent activity Cliff's work stands out because the recollections of a man who has lived through almost all of the last century are bound to have an especial timbre.

Last year, 2007, was the centenary of the Scouts movement of which Cliff was a member from the very earliest days. Other people can give you the facts and figures but with Cliff I can feel the strain of the trek-cart and acrid whiff of campfire smoke. He was there.

Same thing with the Centenary of the Transporter Bridge. People have painted pictures of our principal landmark, measured it, flown under it, rhapsodised about it, cursed it and wanted to sell it to the Americans, neglected and cherished it by turn, but when I wrote about it in 2006, I found no recollection as enlightening as Cliff's. He was born in its shadow, his memory of it going back almost to when its first coat of paint was still wet.

On the many occasions I have telephoned Cliff for information it has arrived after a couple of days together with copious photocopied references and annotations.

The great thing about Forewords is that one can say things that otherwise the subject might wave away as mere flattery.

Light generates warmth.

Within these pages Cliff Knight throws light on myriad subjects and, as a man, exudes a warmth which I feel privileged to have felt.

Mike Buckingham, South Wales Argus, Newport, July 2007

Introduction

Information has been collected from private files of documents gathered by the authors, notes kept over the years and pictures from a range of sources (newspaper and magazine cuttings, family and friends photos, postcards and photographs from previous books etc.). Thanks are expressed to other writers, diarists, local historians, individuals, library staff and researchers and to individuals who have supplied information, letters and pictures. Many of the photos and information were gathered from the people of Pill and Newport and also from information gathered from working in the planning office in Newport. Also friends, neighbours and church folk have been kind enough to supply information as they remember it. Sometimes interest and information has come from responses to letters in the *Argus* and I would like to thank them for their continued interest in 'Olde Newport', and in particular Mike Buckingham. We would like to thank Mike for writing a Foreword to this book.

This book concentrates on items of local history, people and events, often focusing on the smaller local situation that it is easy to forget but which has significance in the overall picture of our city. Much could be written about individual people and families but some of these have been covered in the four previous books by Cliff Knight and also other authors.

The history of Newport can also be woven into the activities of the churches of our town.

The history of the sportsmen and women and the various sporting clubs would also make a fascinating study.

The rise and fall of the Docks and Newport heavy industry is a study in its own right.

Some of the notable families who have influenced our city would be worthwhile research.

The history of the Newport schools has been written and published including Newport High School, St Julian's High School and Brynglas School and Brynglas House (the Newport Reference Library has all the copies of their school magazines).

In this book, to help put the local history into a wider context, a section of the British and Wider World Events occurring at the same time are summarised for each year under consideration. This is not intended to be exhaustive prose or a photograph catalogue but just a taste of world and local events

The book is divided into chapters covering decades of the period from 1900 to 1949 and the photos are integrated into the text as they occur. Hopefully the dates are matched to the events although some are for an era rather than an exact date. Some of the photographs are impaired due to their age and source but are included, however, since it is important to have them as an historical record.

The sketches have been drawn by co-author Alan Jones.

Authors' Profiles

Cliff Knight

Everywhere you go in Newport people seem either to have known Cliff personally or know of his work or have read his previous books. He was known for his accurate memories of Newport and particularly Pill, where he was brought up 'in the shadow of the Transporter'. He was, in fact, on leaving secondary school employed by Newport Borough Council on the Transporter selling tickets to the working men crossing the bridge to Lysaghts and the docks.

During World War II he served in the Medical Corps and saw wartime action in Europe. He was attached to the 5th Infantry Division and sent to the infamous Maginot Line in France. His next assignment was to support the rearguard defence of Norway and his unit was taken out of Norway before it fell into German hands. So where next? To India, then on to work with the 8th Army in North Africa training in readiness for the invasion of Sicily and the Italian mainland. He said in his usual unassuming way, 'I was there in Sicily, Italy and Anzio, and then we took part in the invasion of Southern France and moved with the troops up through France and into Germany'. There is a book about all these travels and horrific events in its own right but he quietly kept the many memories of war to himself.

On returning to Newport, a rather tired ex-soldier, the pieces of life had to be fitted together again and so the ex-Sergeant Knight was re-employed by the council and placed in the planning department. 'I learned a lot more about Newport during that time. But I already knew a lot about Pill as I was brought up there and Nancy and I lived in Adeline Street in the early stages of our married life'. They both went to Alma Street Baptist Church (now after the redevelopment of the area called Emmanuel) and were active with the young people's work. Cliff was also a Deacon and Elder in the church.

When the Pill area was to be redeveloped Cliff was assigned to be the 'trouble shooter, problem solver and appeaser' with the local community moving out of Pill as their houses were knocked down and rebuilt in a different format and layout.

The housing and street plans were complex and the logistics of moving the people in a set sequence required a clear mind and respect from the community.

Everyone knew Cliff and when they were clearing out their houses in readiness to move many brought photos of events and families and many of these have appeared in Cliff's books (and also other people's books as they requested them).

Many photographs of Newport were also taken and processed by Jan Preece who also has an amazing collection of memorabilia from when he ran the excellent heritage centre in Pill, sadly now closed due to lack of funds. People donating the photos and information were pleased to see their contributions in the previous four volumes of Pill penned by Cliff in his usual thorough and meticulous way. Jan has kindly put a large number of the photographs on the internet.

The sad time of losing his devoted wife and helpmate, Nancy, through cancer was a tragic time in Cliff's life but afterwards he was a great help to others going through a similar experience.

Cliff retired from his council duties in 1982 and was encouraged by councillors and friends to write an account of the early days of Newport and to focus on Pill. As mentioned, he wrote four books about Newport, and was a frequent writer to the *Argus*, usually on historical matters. He also wrote a magnificent book about the lives of the writers of the hymns in 'Christian Hymns' containing 800 hymns. This book has been extensively used and is now distributed by The Evangelical Movement of Wales, Bryntirion, Bridgend.

It is amazing how many photos and newspaper cuttings and details of events in Newport he accumulated (certainly over 3,000) but many have been shared with other writers and publications. These include the major contribution to the book on the Royal Gwent Hospital and St Woolos edited by Brian Peeling in 2004 and of course his contribution to the book on the Transporter Bridge in 2006. His failing mobility meant that he used his volumes of gathered photographs, newspaper cuttings, encyclopaedias and the telephone to keep in touch with events … the computer and internet had not been assimilated by Cliff.

Sadly Cliff died in October 2008 after a very rich and treasured life.

Alan Jones

The contact with the internet etc. has been the task of the other writer, Alan Jones who has acted as the 'legs' for some of the work. Cliff's frequent spells in hospital mean that, after he had recovered enough strength, writing time started again albeit at a slower pace. It is a real godsend that his mind and memory had not faded with time. Although restricted to his home in Malpas he still managed to know everything going on in the town and contributed regularly to the letters in the *Argus*.

This book came about from Cliff's feeling that a chronological sequence of events together with supporting photographs would complement his previous publications, so when Alan returned to Newport after retiring as a Professor of Chemistry in Nottingham it was a good opportunity to share each other's expertise. He and his wife had both been secondary teachers in Newport in the 1960s, Alan in the Newport High School and Brenda in St Julian's Girls High School. The suggestion that Alan made of putting the years in a more global context led to more bookwork and research. We did not want a publication that separated the news from the photographs of the period. We decided that to put the British and world scene at the start of each year could be a useful format that showed up Newport in the light of world events. Emphasis has been on the photographs and events of Newport and less photographs are included for 'the world' as these are often more widespread in various internet sites.

When some areas of Newport news were needing an extra photograph or sketch then Alan got to work with his pens and paint brushes and some such illustrations are included. Also some of the older pictures were very thin and lacking in contrast and computer manipulation was needed.

Happy reading and forgive us for any mistakes you notice … we did our best and enjoyed writing it! Hope you enjoy reading it.

Chapter One

The Start of the 20th Century

*'At this time Newport was no more than a large village on the banks
of the River Usk and famous for its shipbuilding, docks,
exporting of coal, its ancient castle and not much else !'*

An Overview

The population of Newport in 1800 was estimated to be 1,135 residents, by 1850 it was about 19,000. The first horse-drawn 'bus service' started in 1845 by George Masters going from Newport Bridge to Old Town Docks four times a day at a fare of 4*d*. Many people could not afford the fare and preferred to walk the dirty muddy road. Horse-drawn trams were started in 1875. The first electric trams were introduced in 1903 (the last one ran in 1937). Newport in the 1880s was a busy coal exporting port, a thriving docks complex and had healthy ship building and repair yards. It was upon this trade and industry that the town's livelihood depended and which was a foundation for its development.

The world during the 20th century saw many changes and built on the exploits and discoveries of the 19th century. The emerging areas of science and technology, industrialisation and improvement of education all helped to influence the events of the 20th century. Medical science saw many breakthroughs including the discovery and use of penicillin, polio shots, flu jabs, cures for smallpox, inoculations for whooping cough, measles, mumps and others. Medical and dental treatment would show a revolution from being expensive to becoming free to all. This was a period that had not envisaged such a thing as organ transplants, new hearts, causes of lung cancer, AIDS, the pill and LSD.

Smoking tobacco was widespread amongst all groups of people and 'fashionable' in the 20th century. 'Grass' meant the green stuff in the fields, not a drug to be smoked, 'Coke' was a fuel to be burned not a drug to be injected for pleasure and a 'joint' was a piece of meat cooked on Sundays not a small amount of marijuana to be smoked. 'Software' was comfortable clothing and 'hardware' was the name of a shop in which to buy tools and screws. A 'pod' was something a pea grew in and a 'digital watch' might have been construed as someone who looked at their fingers.

Homes did not have the advantages of dishwashers, washing machines, food processors and computers, these were things of science fiction. No one would have known the meaning of DVD, CD, photocopy or VHF. In the period being discussed the family treat might be a visit to the 'Music Hall' or free band concert in the park, later in the period they would be superseded by the 'moving pictures' and cinemas. Cable and Sky TV was not even in the vocabulary until after the period under discussion. Holidays were for the rich and a typical working class family might just afford a charabanc trip to the sea side, the lighthouse or even Barry Island. Many were contented with a bus trip or a picnic in a park.

The motor car and its development would become a major invention and air travel become feasible. The mind-bending items read about in the science fiction and comics of the era, regarding space travel and rockets into space would only become possible in future decades. The adventures in the books of Jules Verne, or in the comics of 'Captain Scarlet' or 'Dan Dare, pilot of the future' would surely not ever be possible, would they?

Homes were mainly heated with coal fires and central heating was not common in houses even at the end of our period under discussion (1900-1949). Heavy bed clothes on the beds and frost on the bedroom windows on Winter nights and watching your breath condense in clouds of mist when in bed, was a commonplace thing. Cooking was largely done on coal fires and later the 'posh' electric or gas stoves were more common. Wash day was always on a Monday and was an all day job.

An old incomplete mangle discovered in the yard of the outhouses of the café at Raglan Castle 2007.

Wash day was always on a Monday and an all day job, firstly lighting the kitchen boiler for the hand washing of the clothes using scrubbing boards and then squeezing out the water with mangles before it was then ready to be 'hung out' if it was sunny, otherwise the large ceiling-mounted clothes lines in the kitchen were used.

Lunch was always a rush job and consisted of Sunday's left over. Dylan Thomas called the meal 'Cold meat and soap suds'. An alternative was 'panaclty' which was a fry up of all the veg, potatoes and meat left over from Sunday, others called it 'bubble and squeak'.

Overseas foods were scarce and their widespread availability in the shops was rare. 'Supermarket' was not in the vocabulary and seemed a fantasy for the daydreamers. Fridges and freezers making year round availability of any foods, that we so much take for granted, would have been unbelievable at the start of the period we are looking at. It should be realised that electricity and gas was not available in all homes. The larger homes of the gentry might have a 'cold store' for keeping blocks of ice to keep foods cool. These would be loaded in the winter when ice was plentiful and kept well insulated during the year to help it to last.

Most terraced houses had only cold water and that was sometimes outside and shared by neighbours at the early part of the century but in the latter period of our study bathrooms and the indoor toilet would replace the communal outdoor 'lav', sometimes shared between a few dwellings. The increased health and hygiene in the post-World War years influenced people's life styles and lengthened life expectancy along with the increased health care and use of medicines. The start of the National Health Service in 1948 (the Act of Parliament was passed in 1946) was revolutionary in the care for the sick, child birth, elderly and the provision of glasses, false teeth and free hospital operations.

The local open space, open fields, wooded areas and parks were the 'sports centres' up until post-World War II times, when many open areas became housing estates.

Education saw a continuing revolution during this period after compulsory school ages were imposed at the end of the previous century, improved school conditions, more thorough training for teachers and the eventual raising of the school leaving age up to 14, then 15. There was an improvement in the quality of the curriculum as initially it only concentrated upon the '3 Rs'. Education was to become free and even education available post-16 and education and training for adults were possible. The education of troops both within the period of their war time conscription and provision after they left the forces made an impact upon general skill and knowledge levels.

Employment in Newport saw many changes during the period with the development of the docks, light and heavy manufacturing industries , like steel making and foundry work. The retail trade, banking and office work were the 'white collar' jobs and school teaching and medicine for those able to afford to go further with their education to get the necessary qualifications. The improvement of the tram and bus routes meant people could travel a bit further for work and the bicycle was also popular as a means of getting to work. Towards the end of our period, i.e. the 1930s and 1940s, transport also meant that even Cardiff could be easily reached and road and rail travel up and down the valleys was possible. The world had become 'smaller' since the overseas travel during war times. The increased clarity of radios in the 1930s and 40s also helped to give a wider perspective on the world to working people. TV came into its own in 1950s and its eventual impact was not appreciated by many. It was a miracle just to see the news in pictures in the cinemas of the time.

The 1900 to 1949 period saw changes comparable to the industrial revolution and later decades would see further changes and some not necessarily for the better.

Families were mutually supporting units and marriage breakdowns were uncommon, but became more common in the wartime and postwar years. The words 'social services', 'marriage counsellors' came into existence in the post-World War II years.

A New Century in Newport

This was an exciting time in Newport and worldwide as the start of the century gave to society a feeling of the dawning of a new era with increasing opportunities for self development. There was euphoria and expectation similar to that experienced at the start of the 21st century in 2000. The coverage of worldwide events was by means of reading the newspapers but there was much excitement locally and in Britain that the world was getting smaller and news from abroad was becoming more accessible by telegraph and telephone. There were new visions and expectations for industry, people, society and families. Some felt that the 20th century would see the start of prosperity and the disappearance of dire poverty, there would be full employment, world peace and worldwide travel. The large steamers, able to cross the oceans and take people to far away places, would be available for everyone and not just read about in the newspaper or the library.

Education for all was a possibility and the treatment of illnesses was being tackled. The new Hospital was 'born' on 3rd April, 1893 when the first dispensary opened in Llanarth Street and it was financed by contributions by subscribers who really formed a local health insurance scheme called the Workman's Fund or later the Gwent Hospitals Contributory Fund. By 1900 the fund was worth approximately £1,000 and paid out most of this to the members requiring treatment in the hospitals. The offices of the fund are still on Cardiff Road opposite the Hospital and still perform the tasks of paying out benefits to its subscribers (in 2006 the fund was over £1,000,000).

The main Royal Gwent Hospital buildings were built and formally opened by Lord Tredegar in 1901. It had six wards and cost £25,000. Its running costs were maintained by voluntary donations and some doctors and medical staff gave periods of their time free of charge. Medicine and surgery was becoming more accessible to the working class men and their families. Malnutrition went hand in hand with poverty and the life expectancy was low. You were 'old' at 40 at the start of the century. Infant mortality was high and midwifery was often unhygienic and a source of infant infection. Increased medical knowledge began particularly after World War I.

There was little financial provision for the poor, elderly, destitute or unemployed people except the 'workhouse' which was a dreaded word. Families unable to pay their way often ended up in them. 'To end up in the workhouse' meant deprivation and often death. People would do anything to keep out of the dreaded place. The 'pop shop' or pawnbrokers were the precursor of the loan shark companies. When people were short of money but still needed the basic provisions to support a family the many 'front room' grocer shops would operate credit, often called 'on the slate'. The 'slate' initially was a piece of slate on which the shopkeeper would write in chalk the amount credited, then when it was paid off, usually on pay day, the 'slate' was wiped clean. You would hear people say 'chalk it up' or 'on the slate' if unable to pay.

The idealistic views of the start of the century were soon to be shattered when the situation was seen through real and less euphoric rose-tinted glasses. There were still class differences, poverty, poor housing, expensive health care and unemployment. Newport saw all these situations. In some areas there were large rich houses and in others less than adequate housing. There were people in opulent horse-drawn carriages passing street beggars and street urchins.

Queen Victoria was still on the throne at the start of the century as she had been for many years. Queen Victoria's popularity among all classes in British society was shown at her Diamond Jubilee in 1897 which was an occasion for great public rejoicing. Queen Victoria died on 22nd January, 1901. Her 63-year reign was the longest in the history of England, up to that time. Her reign was referred to as the Victorian era of British history. This period saw the creation of the middle class in society and the period was marked by a sense of morality and intense nationalism. There had been parties and celebration for the Diamond Jubilee in Newport in 1897. There are still streets and pubs containing her name.

In 1900 there was the 'Newport Treat' for 'children of the poor of the town' and held in the athletic grounds at Rodney Parade. A poem appeared in the *Star of Gwent* newspaper which described the events:

> They come from the street and the alley,
> Clean cottage and comfortless slum,
> Oh! See how they eagerly rally,
> For one day of feasting and fun
>
> Enough of their lives in the sadness,
> The poverty hunger and sin,
> Then let them have one day in gladness,
> To bring the new Century in.

There were a number of coal barons and industrialists in Newport employing poorly paid employees. Coal was a major export from Newport and the coal was brought down by train from the valleys to Newport docks where it was loaded onto ships to be sold overseas. All the trucks and tons of coal entering the docks across Lord Tredegar's land surrounding the docks paid a toll of one penny a ton. He became very rich as a result. Welsh coal was prized as good quality coal for boilers in railway locomotives, ships and power stations and industry as it produced a lot of heat and less smoke and ash. To ensure the coal was evenly distributed in the holds of the ships a team of 'Coal Trimmers' was employed to shovel the piles evenly around as it was unloaded from the cranes. It was a dirty job but an essential and well respected one.

The coal trimmers had a dirty job, but a well respected one. There probably was danger to their health from breathing in the coal dust.

There was a possibility of worldwide travel on large liners for the richer people but the majority of people did not move outside their locality. Some privileged people might afford to go abroad to France for holidays. Most families, if they had any holiday at all, delighted in a day trip on a charabanc. The photograph of the charabanc trip was a 1926 street outing to the seaside.

A family visit to a park for a picnic and the luxury of an ice cream was a common holiday for many. One family reported in a private letter to the author how 'a one penny ice cream was shared between his six members of the family on a trip to a park'.

To allow larger paddle steamers and cargo ships up the river a moving Transporter Bridge was thought a suitable type of bridge to cross between the two halves of Newport and in 1899 the French engineer M. Arnodin visited Newport to survey the possibilities for building such a bridge similar to the one he had engineered in France. The problem for the River Usk was the fact that it had the second largest rise and fall of river level in the world, over 30 ft. This bridge was opened in 1906. It was a great spectacle, and still is, even though it has never paid its way in dues to cross the river.

At the turn of the century some of the rich ladies wore opulent and expensive floor length dresses and had a wardrobe of dresses, whilst many workers had one 'Sunday best' outfit and one workday set of clothes; some did not even have the luxury of a change of clothing. These clothes were often worn, washed, dried in front of the fire and worn again the next day. Many women 'took in washing' for the richer people. The presence of the 'boiler and mangle' in many a kitchen bore this out: clothes hanging on lines, out of windows or on rainy days all around the house. The flat iron heating on the fire in readiness for the job of ironing was commonplace. Mondays and other was days filled the house with steamy damp air some of which condensed on cold outside walls and windows. This warm steamy atmosphere was a good breeding place for germs and TB and bronchial infections amongst the population was not uncommon. School cost about one or two pennies a week, so some weeks when there was no money there was no school for the children of the family.

Begging was not uncommon on the streets and petty theft was also common but if caught the penalty was severe. Many had little schooling and young children at an early age (11 or 12 or less) 'went into service' as a maid or gardener in a large household. For the fortunate this meant some form of training and education, for many it was almost like slave labour. The long hours, heavy workload, little time for leisure and no time to go and see the

A photograph of a Newport school classroom about 1900: Bolt Street School, or as it was called 'the University of Pill' or 'the University of Life'.

family meant you were very much controlled by your employer. You had to be educated to escape these conditions and many used the local libraries as a means of reading and learning new things in a hope of something better.

Self-education was not unknown and the libraries were free. Sunday Schools for children was a means of gaining reading skills and education also. It was reported that in 1890 a new reading room was opened at Temple Street and in the same year the 70-strong men's Bible class opened a library in Portland Street. This was extensively used up until the end of the era under discussion (1949).

One item reported that Tredegar Wharf school had 300 pupils and the school got 'no help from the rates'. Five boys were charged and fined for damaging exercise books. It was a privilege to go to school but it cost a small amount. In 1900, Alexandra infants school closed for a month because of an extensive measles outbreak.

Temple Street Public Library.

It was also reported in the local paper that there were a lot of petty crimes and thefts amongst children. Coal stealing by children, probably sent out by their parents, was causing the police much concern. To help the poor children a Sunday morning breakfast was re-started in churches and one church reported 143 children attended. Soup kitchens were also in use for the whole family. It was reported that 'Pill children were neglected, half starved and barefooted'.

Fuels were costly and most houses were heated by coal or wood. So wood collecting, and coal dust recovery from river banks (Ebbw) was an important source of fuel. People waited for the tide to go out and then scraped the coal dust from the mud flats. The coal dust was a result of washing the coal upstream at the collieries, such as Cwmcarn, and also when the river cut through a thin coal seam. It was a dirty job and the trail of black water from improvised wheelbarrows or sacks led from the river banks to the houses. The coal dust was made into bricks sometimes with the help of a little cement powder and allowed to dry out. These briquettes could then be used or sold.

Religion

Wales had many 'visits' by the presence of God in the form of revivals where the Holy Spirit would move people to a profession of faith and had a transforming effect upon their lives. The previous great revival in Wales was in 1859, but the influence of this had greatly waned and the ministers of the churches had lost the power of God in their preaching and the congregations were becoming liberal in their thinking and wayward in their lifestyles. The upsurge of the new science of psychology and the influence of philosophers like William James and Charles Darwin was having its effects upon the people to an extent that they were becoming more 'rational' and less spiritual. It was hoped that the turning of the century would see a reversal of this trend and a return to more God-centeredness, morality and church going. Although there was a remnant of remembrance of the past glory there was generally a decline in church attendance. Perhaps God again would return in power at the turn of the century. Some 'returning' of His presence in power began to occur in 1904. The churches were still large and congregations were respectably full and Sunday schools well attended.

The country was ready for the 1904 revival that broke down barriers between classes. Whereas the 1895 revival emphasised Bible teaching and prayer and personal devotions, the 1904 revival focused more on the emotions and so was soon dissipated when these ran dry. The revivals largely only affected the non-conformist churches but it was a time of great blessing and the well-being of people meant a happier and more honest and enthusiastic society. The gin houses lost clients and a lot of money and the police cells were remarkably empty on pay days and weekends.

A more complete account of the history of 'Old Newport' is recounted in the four books by Cliff Knight listed in the Bibliography. Some are out of print but available in the reference library in Newport.

Chapter Two

The First Ten Years, 1900-1909

1900

The World Scene, Events and People

- Queen Victoria was still on the throne.
- Queen Elizabeth, the present Queen's Mother was born at St Paul's Waldenbury, Hertfordshire as Elizabeth Angela Marguerite Bowes-Lyon, the ninth of ten children. She was the consort of King George VI (1895-1952) whom she married in 1923. She died on 30th March, 2002.
- Earl Louis Mountbatten, British Admiral and commander was born. He was the great grandson of Queen Victoria and he was assassinated in 1979 by Irish extremists.
- Labour Party was formed and called the 'Labour Representation Committee'.
- Unionists gained a majority at the General Election in Britain.
- Boer War, Mafeking, in the Boer War (1899-1902) was relieved from its state of siege.
- Boer War, Relief of Ladysmith after 118 days siege.
- School leaving age raised to 14.
- The Davis Cup for men's tennis was first contested and won by USA in Massachusetts.
- The Boxer Rebellion occurred in China. It was a protest by the Chinese against foreign influences and a Chinese society arose called the 'Righteous and Harmonious Fists'. It believed that boxing and other magical rituals when adopted meant that the weapons of foreigners could not harm them. They opposed Christianity and killed many missionaries. The uprising was put down and the supporters executed.
- Coca-Cola went on sale in Britain for the first time.

The Local Newport Scene, Events and People

Civic and Political offices
- Mayor was William Brown.
- Population of Newport 62,270 (it was only 1,135 a century earlier in 1800).
- Area of Borough 5,020 acres.
- Member of Parliament was Dr F. Rutherford Harris (Conservative).

Commerce
- Newport Union Offices, Queens Hill opened.
- Tredegar Dry Dock Commercial Road/Mill Parade was being constructed.

People
- Miss Elaine Verney, leading lady at the Lyceum theatre announces from the stage that Mafeking had been relieved. There was much rejoicing and cheers.

Places and Events
- Beechwood Park and its large house opened in Chepstow Road.

Beechwood Park house was built in 1886 and bought by the borough council along with 30 acres of parkland in 1900. The house was purchased from George Fothergill, a tobacco merchant, for £11,000. The house was used as a convalescent home during World War I. Restored in a £4.2m project in 2007.

- Kings Head Hotel in High Street rebuilt.
- St Mary's RC School Queen's Hill opened.
- 'Quiet Woman's Row' off Church Street in Pill was reputed to be the roughest street in Newport consisting of a terrace of run down houses with one stinking communal toilet. Continual fighting amongst the women, many of whom were prostitutes, was well known. A public house called the 'Quiet Woman' had a sign outside it depicting a headless woman indicating she was the only type of woman able to keep silent. (No women's rights then!). The street was named (contrariwise) because it was noisy although the headless woman was quiet.
- Lord Tredegar gives ground known as Ponsford Gardens, off Stow Hill, for Alms Houses to be built for the elderly. Earlier houses were rebuilt and refurbished in 1846 and updated again in 1901.

1901

The British and World Scene, Events and People

- Queen Victoria died on 22nd January aged 81. She reigned for 63 years, the longest of all British monarchs. Edward VII was made King on 24th January.
- Seventh British Census took place.
- The first Municipal crematorium in Britain was opened in Hull. Crematorium Act introduced in 1902.
- The first Borstal Institute for young offenders was opened in the village of Borstal, near Rochester, Kent.
- The 25th American president, McKinley was shot by an anarchist, Leon Czolgosz.
- The first oil was found in Texas.

- King Camp Gillette patented the first safety razor.
- Nobel Prize was first awarded. Alfred Nobel (1833-1896) was a Swedish scientist who invented and manufactured explosives, including dynamite He was horrified to see how his invention was used in warfare so he tried to appease things by donating a vast fortune, the interest of which pays for the Nobel Peace and other prizes, including science and medicine.
- Ragtime was the craze in jazz music.
- The first transatlantic wireless signal, the letter 'S' in Morse code was sent from Cornwall by Marconi to Newfoundland (Dec. 12th). The first actual long distance transmission across water was by Marconi and George Kemp and was across the Bristol Channel from Flat Holm to a receiver on the coast near the cliff top church in Lavernock, near Barry in 1897.

Plaque at Lavernock church which marks the sending of the first wireless message over open sea on 13th May, 1897.

The Local Newport Scene, Events and People

Civic and Political
- The Mayor was Henry John Davis (3rd term in office).
- Member of Parliament was Sir Joseph Lawrence (Conservative).
- Population of Newport 67,290. The official census showed Pill had a population of 13,200.
- The council expressed concern about the dangerous way cyclists rode their machines in Commercial Road (similarly in 2008 the 'mountain bikes' seem to be ridden more on the pavements than the roads!)
- Death of Thomas Cordes, one of the first industrialists in Newport and an influential citizen, he was MP for Monmouth Boroughs 1874-80.
- Newport mourns the death of Queen Victoria, many churches held memorial services including a large gathering of non-conformist churches of Maindee which was appropriately held in Victoria Avenue Methodist Church on 2nd February.

Sir Joseph Lawrence (Conservative) doing his canvassing The banner showed his Political slogan 'Cheer for Lawrence and Prosperity'. His method was rather unusual at the time.

Commerce
- Arcade of shops between High St and Cambrian Road opened.
- A tram ride from one end of town to the centre was only for those who could afford the one penny (1*d*.) fare.

A horse-drawn omnibus in Newport. Horse-drawn carts for traders were a common site up to the end of World War II.

People
- Soldiers return home from the Boer War.

Places and Events
- Clytha School Risca Road erected.
- Lord Tredegar considers buying Newport Castle.
- Corporation Road Presbyterian Forward Movement church hall opens.
- Ping-pong, the forerunner of table tennis played for the first time.
- Number of the inmates of the workhouse, Stow Hill rises to 422.
- The 500th house completed on Marshes estate, the remaining 16 acres were used as Shaftesbury Park.

Health
- The County Hospital (The Royal Gwent) opened by Lord Tredegar. It covered 19 acres at Kings Hill Field, Cardiff Road and opened on 5th August, 1901 (the foundation stone was laid in 1897 by Lord Tredegar). It had accommodation for 100 in-patients. There were separate wards for males and females
- Last of the town wells closed and sealed, it was found to be clogged with drowned rats and had become a source of infection.
- Disused Newport Infirmary, 34 Stow Hill, sold to the School Board for £3,900 (later rebuilt - 1904 - to become St Woolos School, for 500 pupils (Builder W.A. Lintons) at a cost of £11,300). The dispensary building of the hospital still exists.

The opening of the Royal Gwent Hospital.

1902

The British and Worldwide Scene, Events and People

- The Coronation of King Edward VII (aged 59), took place on 9th August. It had been delayed for six weeks because the King needed an emergency appendix operation.
- A.J. Balfour became the British Prime Minister (12th July). He brought in an Education Act which provided for secondary education for all and the number of girls in secondary schools rose.
- Empire Day first celebrated in Britain, on 24th May, later called Commonwealth Day
- The treadmill in British prisons was finally suspended, treadmills were originally used as a method of reforming offenders in prison, and brought in by Sir William Cubit in 1817. Modern 'treadmills' are used for fitness and exercise!
- A stand at Ibrox Park football stadium in Glasgow collapsed during an International match between Scotland and England and 25 people were killed and 517 injured. Another disaster of a collapsed stand at Ibrox Park in 1971 resulted in the loss of 66 lives. Over 200 other fans were injured.
- The Second Boer War (1899-1902) between Britain and, what is now, South Africa ended on 31st May. The 'Second War of Independence' as it was called in Africa, was fought from 1899 until 1902, between the British Empire and the two independent Boer republics of the Orange Free State and the South African Republic or Transvaal. In all, the war had cost around 75,000 lives of which 22,000 were British soldiers (7,792 battle casualties, the rest through disease), 6,000-7,000 Boer soldiers, 20,000-28,000 Boer civilians and perhaps 20,000 black Africans.
- Death of Cecil Rhodes (1853-1902) on 20th March. A region of Southern Africa, Rhodesia, was named after him, it is now the country called Zimbabwe. Rhodes amassed a great fortune most of which he left to found scholarships at Oxford University.
- Volcano of Mount Pelee, French Caribbean, erupted killing about 30,000 people.
- Aswan Dam built to control the waters of the Nile and help to prevent flooding was started in 1899 and continued until 1902, later its height was raised.

The Local Newport Scene, Events and People

Civic and Political
- Mayor was John Holman Dunn.
- Charles Thomas elected as first Labour Councillor.
- Monmouthshire County Council offices opened in Pentonville (11th June) at a cost of £9,000.
- Coronation of Edward VII celebrations and an Avenue and a Crescent in Newport were named after him.

Almost every recent King or Queen has a road, street or avenue named after them, such as King Edward the VII Crescent and Avenue.

Commerce
- East Usk power station was built at Corporation Road.
- Tredegar Dry Dock opened at the junction of Commercial Road and Mill Parade in Pill.
- Tenders were accepted and construction began on the Transporter Bridge.

People
- Head teacher R.L. Davies of Alexandra Road Boys School had a salary of £240 pa and E. Jones in the corresponding Girls school received £120 pa.
- 400 pupils from Alexandra Girls school, Pill, and the infant school went to the lighthouse for the afternoon in a series of horse-drawn brakes as a special outing.

Places and Events
- New 4th Battalion South Wales Borderers Drill Hall in Dock St opened by Lord Raglan.
- Wesleyan Church, St Julian's Avenue opened.
- Lliswerry school rebuilt (first erected 1879).
- Corporation Road School erected for 628 boys, 534 girls and 458 infants.

Health
- Concern expressed about the spread of Tuberculosis (TB). It was reported that there were 62 deaths from the disease in Newport in 1901. Five cases of smallpox in Lime Street. Two deaths, one at the Port Sanitary Hospital, Mendalgief Road.
- Fresh air was thought to be the answer to many diseases. There was probably some truth in this as the sanitary conditions of houses and communal toilets and the impurity of some of the drinking water wells all contributed to illness. Water sellers sold pure water but it was 'expensive' for the ordinary household.
- Public baths and swimming baths were opened in a few places in Newport including Stow Hill and Pill. The Pill baths was not a success and eventually closed.

1903

The British and Worldwide Scene, Events and People

- Ministerial government crisis in Britain. Many members resign from the government.
- The first municipal motor bus service in the world was inaugurated in England between Eastbourne station and Meads, Sussex.
- Workers Education Association (WEA) was formed in Britain.
- The British newspaper the *Daily Mirror* was published in London.
- In USA the first controlled flight in a 'heavier than air' powered machine was made by the Wright brothers (Orville 1871-1948 and Wilbur 1867-1912) at Kitty Hawk, North Carolina on 17th December.

The Local Scene, Events and People

Civic and Political
- Mayor was Col W. Clifford Phillips.
- Death of Henry John Davis, highly respected citizen. Mayor three times and he gave much support to the building of the County Hospital, Cardiff Rd (The Royal Gwent Hospital).
- A proposal to run trams on Sundays was rejected.
- Last horse-drawn trams seen on the streets of Newport, being replaced by electric ones. Use of motor omnibuses were also being considered for the future.

Commerce
- Electric Tram Service started. Corporation, Chepstow, Caerleon, Commercial and Malpas Roads electrified with overhead cables. First electric tram from Pill Gates to Lysaghts at a cost of two pence (2*d*). Electric trams ran until 1937 in Newport.
- Queen Victoria Alms houses opened at the top of Stow Hill to replace those erected 60 years before. Cost £2,500.
- Redundant Newport Tramway horses sold at the Cattle Market with prices ranging from £7 to £35 (May).
- Exports and imports at Alexandra Docks reached half a million tons, a record year.
- West Park laundry , Preston Avenue, opened.
- Ferdinand Joseph Arnodin, the French designer of the Transporter Bridge, visits the site in Newport to see the start of the construction.

Mr Arnodin, visited the Transporter site to view the development of the foundations and initial structures of the innovative bridge.

A photograph of the progress in 1904 and 1905 on the footings of the Transporter Bridge.

People
- Five pupils were fined for stealing books, pencils from Bolt Street School.
- The well-known George Travers of Pill Harriers Rugby Club gained the first of his 25 international caps for Wales.
- Councillor Gower, a Pill Liberal Councillor, told the council of a house in his ward which had one room on the first floor which could only be reached by a ladder. There were no beds and the occupants had to sleep on straw. He asked the council to consider building 66 houses for the working class, but the council rejected his scheme.

Places and Events
- Commercial Road Baptist church in Pill had a membership of 505 adults and a Sunday school of 663.
- Some houses in Newport sold for as little as £130.
- Sailors Rest Home opened at Alexandra Road.
- Wild West Show at Shaftesbury Park had 700 men and 500 horses.
- Penylan Baptist Mission Church was established at Christchurch, the foundation stones for its buildings were later laid in 1914 by Messrs Blow and Rosser.

Health
- Newport Workhouse, Stow Hill (later St Woolos Hospital) completed. Padded rooms installed for troublesome inmates.
- *South Wales Argus* raised £1,762 towards the new Hospital (Royal Gwent).

Allt-yr-yn Isolation Hospital.

- Infectious Disease Isolation Hospital at Allt-yr-yn extension opened. When children were admitted they were not allowed to see their parents until they were discharged.

- Foundation stone of the Newport Asylum was laid at St Cadoc's Mental Hospital, Caerleon.

St Cadoc's Hospital: its foundation stone was laid in 1902 and opened in 1903.

1904

The British and Worldwide Scene, Events and People

- The first motor vehicle registration plate in Britain was issued to Earl Russell for his 'Napier'.
- France and Britain sign a treaty called the 'Entente Cordiale' to help bring the two countries closer together in political and social understanding.
- The Football Federation (FIFA) was founded in Paris.
- Sir Henry Morton Stanley, the world famous explorer, died.
- The CQD distress call sign was introduced. The CQ meant 'seek you' with D added for danger. It was later replaced by SOS in 1906.
- The first main line electric train in UK left Liverpool for Southport.
- Work began on the 40 mile-long Panama Canal. It was opened to shipping on 15th August, 1914.
- The third Olympic games opened at St Louis, Missouri, USA.

The Local Scene, Events and People

Civic and Political
- Mayor was Robert Wilkinson.
- Population of Newport was 71,378 in 12,000 dwellings.
- New road bridge opened at Bridge St over the railway.

- Trams start running over Newport Bridge to Maindee.
- Memorial tablet to Newport soldiers who fought in the Boer War was hung in the Town Hall by Lord Tredegar.
- The council enact a by-law restricting the speed of motor cars to 10 miles per hour in the town area.

Commerce
- Wentwood Waterworks Reservoir opened, cost £39,000, capacity 41,000 gallons.
- Town Dock, (constructed in 1835-1842, opened in 1842 and extended in 1858), was considered obsolete for the large ocean steamers and the manager, Mr McCauley decided to turn it into an import dock for general cargo. The dock was extended in 1907.

People
- Dr Wrenford, beloved minister of St Paul's Church in Commercial St for nearly 50 years, died. He lived in a house at the bottom of Belle Vue Lane which was later demolished and the land incorporated into Belle Vue Park. Revd J.T.Wrenford developed a friendship with the famous hymn writer Miss Havergal when she visited Newport and was sent a copy of the Hymn, 'Take my life and let it be consecrated Lord to Thee' for his comments before it was published.

> *Take my life and let it be,*
> *Consecrated, Lord to thee;*
> *Take my moments and my days,*
> *Let them flow in ceaseless praise*

- A shopkeeper was fined for Sunday trading.
- Four boys were fined for playing 'pitch and toss', a gambling game, in George Street.

Places and Events

Carnegie Library is still in use in 2007. It is next to Corporation Road School which made it a great resource to pupils and teachers over the years.

- Andrew Carnegie, a United States industrialist, gives £2,000 for the building of a free library at Corporation Road. This still bears his name. It was opened in 1907.
- Welsh Christian spiritual revival felt in Newport. New Churches started and older ones were 'revived' and became full again.
- Bowling green at Newport Athletic ground, Rodney Parade started and opened later in 1905.
- Newly-built Kings Head Inn High Street changes its name to Kings Head Hotel.
- Tidal wave lands at Newport, parts of Caerleon submerged.

Sketch of Hanbury Arms Caerleon by Alan Jones. It would be interesting to know how the tidal wave effected Caerleon.

- Welsh Lawn Tennis Championships held at the Newport Athletic grounds, Rodney Parade. Americans beat the Australians in the final.
- Baptist Church, Llanthewy Road opened; cost £3,000.
- Corporation Road Baptist Church (established in 1898) and a new building was started in 1904; they had 610 children with 51 teachers (this rose to 906 children and 65 teachers by 1922).
- The May Festival held at the Temperance Hall, Dock Street.
- St Luke's Church opened in Bridge St.
- St Woolos School, Stow Hill erected on old infirmary site, and opened in 1905 with 480 boys, 478 girls, 244 infants.
- St Basil's Church, Bassaleg was restored and re-opened.

Left: St Basil's Church, Bassaleg.   Right: St Luke's Church, just before demolition in 2008.

- Alexandra Rd Baptist Church, Pill, was bought by a deacon of Alma Street Baptist church but continued to function as a church.

Alexandra Road Baptist Church. When it closed it was successfully used as a History and Local Museum run by Jan Preece and his wife. It closed in 2006 due to lack of finances to purchase the building from the Baptist Union.

- Beechwood Bowling club at Beechwood Park was formed and is still in existence in 2008.

Health
- The local churches provided £260 towards the Newport & Mon Hospital (Royal Gwent) and a sixth ward opened. Each year the Newport Churches held a 'Hospital Sunday' where the collections went to the Hospital for upkeep. Often the medical members of staff used to visit the churches to take up the collection.
- Maternity Home opened in Herbert Street, Pill. This was the first in Newport to train midwives.

1905

The British and Worldwide Scene, Events and People

- Thomas Barnado, an Irish doctor and philanthropist, died.
- 'Aliens Act 'introduced in Britain to help the Home Office control Immigration.
- Sir Henry Irving (1838-1905) died. He was a famous actor and theatrical manager.
- 'Red' or 'Bloody' Sunday massacre at St Petersburg, Russia (20th January) when at least 500 people were slaughtered as thousands marched on the Winter Palace of the Tsar to protest about Nicholas II's reign.
- The Rotary Club was formed in offices in Dearborn, Chicago by Arthur Griffith.
- Albert Einstein (1879-1955) introduced his 'Special Theory of Relativity' to the world of Science.

The Local Scene, Events and People

Civic and Political
- Mayor was John Liscombe.
- Godfrey Morgan (Lord Tredegar), a most generous benefactor to the town was made a Viscount.
- Rogerstone Free library opened.
- Pillgwenlly Police station moved from Temple Street to Alexandra Rd near the docks entrance.
- Tredegar Estate offices at Queens Hill opened for administration and land rent collection. Became a listed building.

Tredegar Estates Office, Fields Road.

Commerce
- A new East Quay of the Southern Docks opened at Alexandra Docks.
- New bowling green opened in Belle Vue Park in June.

People
- Harry Houdini (1874-1926) performed at the Lyceum, Bridge Street and escaped from Newport Police cells as a stunt. He performed many escapes from seemingly impossible positions. He eventually died, not due to a stunt, but from appendicitis. His real name was Ehrich Weiss, an American citizen, born in Budapest, Hungary.
- A 9-year-old boy was charged by the police for throwing stones.

Places and Events
- New Presbytery built at St Mary's RC church, Stow Hill.
- 2,400 children attend the poor children's treat at the Newport Athletic club. It was reported that most children had poor and ragged clothing, but clean.
- Seamen's new Institute in Ruperra Street, Pill opened.

Health
- Royal Gwent Hospital had an X-ray room installed. (This was quite innovatory as it was only 10 years after X-rays had been discovered. Roentgen received the Nobel prize for his discovery in 1901.)

The Spiritual Revival 1904/05

- Spiritual Revival meetings at a number of Newport churches occurred during 1904/5. Some of the reports from church records give the following insights to the revival.
- Commercial Road Baptist church, meetings started as an open air meeting on the steps outside the church followed by an enthusiastic meeting inside and several went to the 'inquiry room' after the meeting.
- Revival meetings at the Ebenezer Welsh Church at the junction of Commercial Road and Ebenezer Terrace.
- Services were held most days of the week including Saturday morning. Many confess to having been 'born again' during enthusiastic packed meetings. Congregation join in prayer in both Welsh and English. In one meeting half the congregation made a profession of faith in Christ. One meeting closed at 9.30 pm and the whole congregation went out into the street and formed a procession and marched down Commercial Road singing hymns. They were joined by the young men from YMCA and a strong contingent from Commercial Road and Alma Street Baptist churches. The long procession marched to Temple Street where an open air meeting took place and short addresses were given by Mr Lennard followed by prayers and revival hymns. They then were led back in procession by Revd D.H. Williams, minister of Ebenezer Church and they then ended with prayer and praise. The *Argus* faithfully reported all the news of the revival meetings in colourful and descriptive language so that readers could almost get the enthusiasm and flavour of the various events.

Alma Street Baptist Chapel.

1906

The British and Worldwide Scene, Events and People

- There was a Liberal landslide majority in the British General Election.
- Kier Hardie, a Labour MP, elected for the first time, in the constituency of Aberdare, South Wales. A memorial was unveiled at Aberdare in 2006 to commemorate this historic event. He led the Labour Party and steered away from Marxism to a more Christian form of Socialism. Although he was brought up as an atheist, Hardie was converted to Christianity and became a lay preacher at the Evangelical Union Church. Christianity became an important influence in his political career.

- In 1908, Hardie resigned as leader of the Labour Party and spent the rest of his life campaigning for votes for women. He died in Glasgow in 1915 after a series of strokes.
- Movement for women's suffrage became active in Britain.
- Free School Meals for poor children introduced.
- The Cunard liner *Mauretania* was launched on the River Tyne, she was the holder of the Blue Riband for the fastest crossings of the Atlantic for over 20 years. The *Mauretania* ended her voyages in September 1934.
- The weekly magazine *John Bull* first published.
- Rolls-Royce Ltd started as a car company. They decided to make a distinctive feature of the radiator of their cars and struck on the idea to replicate the classical shape of the Greek Temple of Athena and to have 'the Spirit of Ecstasy' as the radiator top mascot.
- England won the first Rugby International against France.
- The San Francisco earthquake and resulting fire started just before dawn resulting in 452 deaths (18th April), but it was later suggested this was a gross underestimation and more likely to have been several thousands. More than half the population of 400,000 were left homeless.
- Wilbur Wright patented his aeroplane design.

The Local Scene, Events and People

Civic and Political
- The Mayor was Frederick Phillips. He was made an Alderman in 1910. He was a member of the family which established Phillips Brewery in Dock Street. He was a fine sportsman and a lifelong member of Newport Athletic club. He was made a Freeman of the Borough in 1936.
- Lewis Haslam (Liberal) was elected for the first time as Member of Parliament.
- An earthquake was felt in the town but with little damage and no casualties.
- Newport Police force learnt 'Jiu-jitsu' as a means of self defence.
- The Newport Library staff were instructed to black out the racing pages on newspapers in the library to discourage gambling.
- The Transporter Bridge was opened in Brunel Street, Pill by Lord Tredegar (12th September). The cost of the bridge was £98,000. 1,300 passengers travelled free on the first day. In the first 4½ days 43,000 people went over it. Charges were ½d. or 1d. first class and 2d. for a large animal. Takings were £90 for this period.

Commerce
- Marks & Spencer opened a store in High Street Arcade.
- The digging of the deep water entrance to Alexandra Docks was started.
- The Alexandra Docks and Railway Company started a motor bus service.

People
- Children had lessons in temperance in school.
- Three young boys charged with stealing coal. One lad with previous convictions was given six strokes of the birch.

People used to ponder if it would be safe to ride on and if the cables broke would the gondola float? Some people called it the 'Flying Ferry'. The Newport Pictorial said in 1906 'This ingenious design is one of the most remarkable and interesting of the later public improvements of the Town'.

Transporter Bridge towards the end of its mammoth construction. The filming of the opening took place in September 1906: this was the first time filming of moving pictures that was undertaken in Newport and they were shown in the Empire Theatre, Charles Street the next day.

Viscount Tredegar at the opening of the Transporter.

The first crossing of the Transporter by Viscount Tredegar and dignitaries.

- Charles Pritchard captained Newport RFC for three seasons (1906-9), won 14 caps for Wales and died in World War I. One generous act typical of the man was when he was chosen for Wales and his friend, Ernie Jenkins, was chosen as first reserve (Charlie had already been capped, Ernie had not), so Charlie told the selectors he was unfit so that Ernie could get his first cap.

Places and Events

Mr Sully who was the berthing master at Rodney Parade landing stage with his prize winning model yachts which he often sailed in Shafesbury Park.

- Model Yacht club started at Shaftesbury Park.
- Durham Road school opened for 368 pupils.
- National School opposite St Paul's Church, Commercial Street was closed.
- The Central Hall, Commercial Street (opposite St Paul's Church) was opened. (It was closed in 1960.) It was for many years used as a place of worship and the large building was used for performances by many of the world famous orchestras, choirs and talented musicians. It was said to be the first building in Newport to show 'moving pictures'. Seating 1,800 people, the building was offered to the Newport Council in 1962 but they declined the offer to keep it open and it was sold for shops.
- Great Western Railway motor car service starts running.
- Beechwood Park Presbyterian Church was established in the lecture hall, Chepstow Road. Church building rebuilt in 1922.
- Foundation stone for St Barnabas Church, Ruperra Street, Pill laid and church opens. Cost £1,810. The site was given by Lord Tredegar.

Health

- Cost of treating a patient at Newport and Mon Hospital (Royal Gwent) was £1 per hour. The first Royal Gwent Hospital fete in Belle Vue Park raised £80.
- Newport 'Asylum' was opened on 25th January (St Cadoc's Mental Hospital, Caerleon) at a cost of £150,000. It could accommodate 368 inmates.
- Springfield Mansion near the Workhouse was used to house highly contagious TB patients. As part of their treatment the able-bodied were encouraged to work and use the 4/5 acres of land to grow vegetables for the institution to feed the patients. The open air was thought to help recuperation.
- Serious allegations and a petition by 420 residents said that Pill people were being poisoned by the smell from the sewers. Pure water and good hygienic sanitary conditions were still a rarity for most working class families. It was safer to drink ale rather than local water. Often acceptably clean drinking

water was only available from communal water pumps or bought from water sellers from carts going around an area. As the population and industry increased so did the requirements for more water and projects were frequently discussed in council meetings of building more water storage and more reservoirs.

1907

The British and Worldwide Scene, Events and People

- The Boy Scout movement was originated on an experimental camp held on Brownsea Island, Dorset by Robert Baden Powell.
- Florence Nightingale was presented with the Order of Merit by King Edward VII for her work during the Crimean War. Her training and hygiene techniques saved many lives. After the war in 1860 she set up a training programme for nurses in St Thomas's hospital in London. This was the start of professional training for nurses.
- The Central Criminal Court, known as the Old Bailey, was opened by King Edward VII on the site of Newgate prison (27th January).
- School medical system started.
- The first Isle of Man motorcycle TT race was held, Rem Fowler won the first TT race on a 672cc Norton at an average speed of 42.9 mph.
- The Territorial Army, a British volunteer force, was established.
- The first taxicabs fitted with meters started operating in London.
- Mother's Day was initiated in America by Miss Anna Jarvis.
- Norman Brookes, an Australian, became the first 'overseas' tennis player to win the men's Wimbledon tennis singles title. For the previous 30 years it was won by British players. Since then only two British players have won the men's singles title at Wimbledon, Fred Perry and Arthur Gore.

The Local Scene, Events and People

Civic and Political
- The Mayor was Thomas Parry, JP.
- Carnegie Free Library opened in Corporation Road on 14th March, 1907.
- Bath & West of England show visited Newport again and used the site near the Old Manor House, St Julian's, Caerleon Road.
- The Prince of Wales visited Newport.

Commerce
- Shipping trade increases in Alexandra Docks. Finance for an extension of the Docks was being considered in a Bill before Parliament.
- John Lysaght works issued a High Court writ against the Council for £7,500 for loss of access to their East bank works but the council settled out of court.

The tram driver and conductor and fare collector were issued with uniforms. They differed in the colour of the hat tops. The silver attachment around the conductor's chest was the machine for clipping the ticket so that it could not be used again. The tickets were kept in a small hand rack and the colours of the tickets showed the price that was paid. Some people and children collected the tickets as mementos of their trips.

- Tram drivers and conductors were issued with uniforms for the first time.
- On Easter Monday 11,300 people crossed by the Transporter Bridge and 968 people walked over the top.
- For the first year of use of the Transporter 390,318 people crossed the bridge producing revenue of £1,331 7s. 1d.

People
- 18-year-old Ada Hatherway attempts suicide by jumping off the gondola on the Transporter Bridge. Over the years many people have either jumped from the top or the gondola attempting to commit suicide.
- Newport Councillor Peter Wright, a renowned world wrestler, took on George Hackensechendt, the world champion, in a charity event with money going to suitable causes.
- Peter Wright commended for his bravery as he stopped a runaway horse and cart in Chepstow Road.
- A Mrs Boyles of South Market Street, mother of 22 children (19 of whom had died), was in court for non payment of debts.
- John Davies of Commercial Road was summoned for frequenting and loitering for the purpose of bookmaking and gambling.
- Albert Fear was born in Abertillery (he died in 2000). He played for Newport Rugby club 86 times and Wales in 1934-5. He was said to be a 'fearless' wing forward. The mother of the famous outside half, Cliff Jones, wrote to Albert Fear after the Welsh game with Scotland and said, 'I want to thank you for looking after my son against the Scottish forwards'. This letter was treasured by Albert and the family.

Places and Events
- The Lyne Road reading room moved to Shaftesbury Street.
- Shipping trade increased in Alexandra Docks and a Parliamentary Bill was passed to raise more capital for a further extension to it.
- There was a proposal before the council to widen Cardiff Road at the bottom of Belle Vue Lane.
- Emmanuel Congregational Church, London Street, build a new church alongside the old one which was built in 1892.
- Railway disaster at the Ebbw Bridge Junction, Maesglas, 29th September.
- The Savoy Hotel and Silver Grill, High Street, was under construction.
- Cromwell Road Primitive Methodist Church opened at Somerton.
- New Post Office in High Street opened between the station approach and the Corn Exchange. Cost about £3,000.

The house on the right-hand side is on the corner of Cardiff Road and Capel Crescent. A railway line went along in front of the houses. A level crossing is just visible alongside the house.

Spectators at the scene of the Maesglas railway accident.

Heavy lifting gear moving the derailed train.

Post Office on the corner of Station Approach, close to the Corn Exchange.

Health
- The first endowed bed given to the Royal Gwent Hospital in the will of the well known ship owner, C.H. Bailey. Many more were later donated and are listed in the 1948 History of the Hospital (*see Bibliography*).
- Mayor appealed for people to give generously as the Hospital was £1,248 in debt.
- The Workhouse (now St Woolos Hospital) recognised for the training of midwives.

1908

The British and Worldwide Scene, Events and People

- Asquith becomes Prime Minister of British Parliament.
- The fourth Olympic games held in London.
- 56 runners took part in the London Marathon.
- England played its first International soccer game against an overseas country winning 6-1 against Austria in Vienna.
- Winston Churchill, then 34, married Clementine Hozier; the marriage lasted 56 years.
- The first aeroplane flight in England was made at Farnborough in Hampshire by an American, Samuel Cody. He reached 1,390 ft. Observers from the War office decided that there was no future in this sort of plane.
- The first international beauty contest in Britain was held in the Pier Hippodrome, Folkestone.
- Britain's first lady was elected as Mayor in Alderburgh Suffolk.
- Juvenile courts first established.

- First Ford model 'T' motor car rolled off the production line at Detroit, USA. This was the beginning of the 'cheap' motor cars.
- FBI, Federal Bureau of Investigation, was set up in America.
- Jack Johnson (1878-1946) became the first coloured boxer to win a world heavyweight title.
- Messina, on the Island of Sicily was seriously damaged by an earthquake and 156,500 lives were lost (28th December). The same terrible earthquake destroyed a great part of Calabria in south-west Italy.

The Local Scene, Events and People

Civic and Political
- The Mayor was Graham William White, JP.

Commerce
- Strike by Dock labourers (March).
- Marked increase in coal exports at Alexandra Docks.
- 187,760 people used the Transporter Bridge, almost half the number from the previous year.

People
- St Michael's baseball team, Pill, formed 1908/9.
- Three Newport hockey players represent Wales at the Olympic Games.
- Death of William Grant, who was a well known Bible scholar and writer of many poems dealing with local events.

Places and Events
- The Wesleyan Chapel, Commercial Road, was gutted by fire.
- It was reported that theft and assaults were common in the Pill area.

Health
- Expenditure at the Newport and Mon (Royal Gwent) Hospital doubles. 40 per cent of its income was supplied by the local churches.
- Maternity Home in Herbert Street, Pill opens, the first maternity home in Newport.
- The Workhouse (later the site of St Woolos Hospital) equipped with a 200-bed infirmary. Able-bodied people were expected to work for their living. Even though pensions were given in 1909 this still fell below the amount needed to feed and keep a family. Any poor people not able to pay their bills were 'put in the poor house or workhouse' This was a dreaded route for any family as there was no privacy, families were either separated or squashed into poor accommodation and hygiene was poor, consequently disease and infection was rife. The fear of the name 'Workhouse' hovered over the head of the Woolaston House Hospital and many patients were almost afraid to go there fearing that the stigma of the 'workhouse' would remain on them.
- The Burton Homes, Friars Road near Belle Vue Park, opened to accommodate 12 females. Erected by Col Henry Burton and his brother.

Burton homes as they still stand in 2008, behind the top of Belle Vue Park.

1909

The British and Worldwide Scene, Events and People

- The first payment of the Old Age Pensions' were made in Britain (1st January). They were five shillings to persons over 70.
- Selfridges, the American-owned departmental store, opened in London.
- The first Woolworths store opened in Lord's Street, Liverpool.
- Rail and coal miners strike.
- Louis Bleriot (1872-1936) the French aviator became the first man to fly across the English Channel (25th July) from Calais to Dover in a monoplane of his own design.
- Union of South Africa was formed.
- Commander Robert Peary (1856-1920), the US polar explorer, became the first person to reach the North Pole. Peary wrote: 'The Pole at last! The prize of 3 centuries, my dream and ambition for 23 years. *Mine* at last …' His claims were disputed as he had no one trained in navigation to confirm it and his camera was a primitive one and was lost. But it is believed that his mistakes were honest ones. The claims of Federick Cook that he had reached the pole the year before was a matter of dispute as he also had no proof of his exact position.
- The British Antarctic Expedition led by Earnest Shackleton reached latitude 88° 23' South by their overland trip which was just 97 miles short of his goal. His trip was well documented and its navigation logs were kept accurately. He turned back because his men were exhausted. He died of a heart attack on an expedition in 1922.

The Local Scene, Events and People

Civic and Political
- Mayor was William Miles Blackburn. He was a builder and had constructed Alexandra Rd Baptist Church, St Stephen's, St Michael's churches and others.
- The Rt Hon. Godfrey Charles Morgan, Lord Tredegar, received the Freedom of the Borough on 9th June and Alderman John Moxon was also granted the Freedom of the Borough.

Commerce
- Serious fire at Basham's drapery shop, Commercial Road.

- Death of J.M. Griffiths head of Griffiths Bros, Clothiers was reported. The firm was founded by his mother in a front room in a house in Dolphin St in 1870. They had a few shops and a factory in George Street.

Griffiths & Sons' transport and delivery van about 1910.

Alexandra Dock during construction with a large trench propped up with wooden supports.

Tom (Toya) Lewis, 'The Little Hero'.

Some of the team of diggers helping to recover trapped workers. There is a Wetherstone Café in Newport at the corner near St Paul's Church named after Tom Toya Lewis.

J.M. Griffiths' workshops in Commercial Road. Its large premises in Commercial Road was knocked down in 1978.

- The tea room at Belle Vue Park opened in November. The restored building is a very good representation of the original as the two photographs show.

Belle Vue Park's Tea Rooms: original and restored (2007).

People
- Jack Morley, one of the finest wings ever to play for Newport RFC and Wales was born. He became a dentist by profession and turned 'professional' for the Wigan rugby league club in 1932. He died in March 1972.
- Peter Wright (local councillor and mayor in 1919) won the Middleweight Wrestling Championship of UK.
- Tom 'Toya' Lewis , aged 15, risked his life trying to save the trapped men at Alexandra Dock when a dug trench collapsed. He received the Albert Medal for his bravery from the King. A mass grave was constructed at St Woolos churchyard for the 39 victims of the docks disaster and their names were carved on a memorial in the graveyard.

Places and Events
- The foundation stone of the new YMCA building in Commercial Street near Palmyra Place was laid and the building constructed at a cost of £8,293.
- Electric lighting installed in St Woolos Church.

Chapter Three

Traumatic Years, 1910-1919

This chapter will deal with a traumatic period in the history of the country, Europe and the world. It starts and ends with peace but the intervening years of the middle of the decade saw the most horrific carnage the 'civilised world' had ever known. The 'Great War' of 1914-18, as it was then called, affected every household, street, village, town and social class. Everyone knew of family, friends or relatives that had been killed either in 'the Flanders fields' or other areas of warfare. This is not to belittle the enormity of its effects but this book will not dwell on the war details but seek to use a more local perspective of the times. The history of the war is left to other authors and their publications.

The decade also saw the emergence of some new nations created either by revolution such as Latvia and Lithuania and others were proclaimed republics such as Austria, Czechoslovakia and Chile.

There was a growing awareness of the need for giving educational opportunities to a wider group of people other than those privileged to be able to afford high school fees. The Balfour Education Act of 1904 and the creation of an opportunity for secondary education, access to higher education and the improved training for teachers all prepared the way for a broadening of education for the general population. There were developing opportunities for women to enter higher education and also the fee-paying grammar schools were offering free scholarships. The number of girls entering higher education was still low but it did open up opportunities for them to become 'pupil teachers' and give them an opportunity to see if they wanted to progress to further training establishments (if they could afford it as higher education was not free). The Fisher Education Act of 1918 proposed that all pupils were entitled to secondary education up to the age of 14 (previously it was 12) with schooling of 320 hours a year (eight hours a week). This took until 1921 to be fully implemented. The secondary school curriculum would now include practical work and science and languages were introduced as were examinations in 1911.

One elderly lady in her nineties, born during this period, informed these authors that she,

… would have loved to be educated further as I was good at most subjects in school and excelled in Art, English and mathematics but my parents could not afford to keep me in school beyond 14. My father was an engine driver with GWR and my mother took in washing to eke out the family finances. The staff in school (Municipal Secondary School) were rather disparaging also and could not understand why a 'Pill girl' from humble background would want to go to college as people would laugh at me. So I found work in A.T. Morgan general clothiers and milliners as the cashier, where I was very happy. I did have the joy of helping my son with his English and French home work and realised I could at least have been a 'pupil teacher'. I also had the joy of seeing my son progress through secondary education in the 1940-50s to higher education where he gained a BSc. He was one of the first generation of graduates in our family and only because it was free.

1910

The British and Worldwide Scene, Events and People

- King Edward VII died and was succeeded by his son George V (6th May). George V was the second son of Edward VII but succeeded to the throne as his older brother, Albert Victor, died in 1892.
- Liberals win two General Elections in succession.
- There were more than 100 arrests when suffragettes tried to storm the House of Commons.
- Labour party demand the abolition of the House of Lords.
- Dr Crippen the mass murderer was caught by the use of a radio telegraph to the ship on which he was travelling to Canada, SS *Montrose*, as he tried to escape. He was brought back to Britain, tried and hanged at Pentonville prison on 23rd November.
- Florence Nightingale, 1820-1910, the English nurse in the Crimean War and founder of modern nursing, died in London aged 90. In 1851 she founded the Nightingale School and Home for nurses, in London.
- There was a rail and miners' strike.
- Halley's comet appeared in the sky. It appears in the sky every 76 years and is probably the most well-known comet. It appeared, and is recorded in 1066 and also features in many ancient paintings as it was considered to be a very mysterious object until Edmond Halley explained what it really was. It consists of porous rock filled with ice and as it approaches the sun's heat in its elliptical orbit some of the ice sublimes and we see it as a 'tail'.
- The first person in Britain to get a pilot's licence issued by the Royal Aero Club was J.T.C. Moore Brabazon, later to become famous as Lord Brabazon of Tara (1884-1964). He designed the world's largest plane but it was a financial disaster and did not go into production.
- Manchester United played their first league game at Old Trafford.
- Canberra officially became the capital of Australia.
- Samuel Langhorne Slemens, or pen name Mark Twain, died, he wrote the story of *The Adventures of Tom Sawyer* and *Adventures of Huckleberry Finn*.
- Mother Teresa (born Agnes Gonxha Bojaxhiu) of Calcutta was born in Albania. Mother Teresa was a Roman Catholic nun, dedicated to the relief of the poor in India. She was a Nobel Prize winner for Peace in 1979. She died in 1997.
- Madame Marie Sklodowska Curie (born in 1867) isolated a few grams of the radioactive element radium from tons of pitchblende ore. Her work along with her husband Pierre Joliot was a major contribution to science and led to the medical use of radiation treatments for cancers. She is the only woman to receive two Nobel prizes, one in Chemistry and one in Physics, shared with her husband Pierre Joliot. She herself died of cancer in 1934.
- Charles Stewart Rolls, 1877-1910, was killed in an air crash in Bournemouth, being the first person to die in an air crash. His monument is in Monmouth town centre. He is buried in Llangattock churchyard.

A statue of Charles Stewart Rolls stands in a square in Monmouth, in his hands he is holding a model of a biplane. He was killed in an air crash at Bournmouth. He was the first British pilot to die in a plane accident. He is buried in Llangattock churchyard, just outside Monmouth.

Rolls was the first man to fly across the English Channel and back, non stop in 1910.

He along with Frederick Royce were the co founders of the prestigious car and engineering firm Rolls-Royce in 1904 and in 1906 and created the first Rolls-Royce Silver Ghost car.

He was also famous for his motoring skills and won many prizes and broke many records. He was responsible for changing the speed limit on public roads from 4 mph to 12 mph.

The Local Scene, Events and People

Civic and Political
- Mayor was John Henry Williams.
- Town Clerk was A.A. Newman, he was the youngest person to be appointed to the position at the age of 22 in 1882 but he faithfully served in the post for over 40 years.
- Member of Parliament was Lewis Haslam (Labour).
- The Council borrowed money to buy Coronation Park near the Transporter Bridge.
- The town motto was chosen to be *Terra Marque* (Land by the sea).
- Council installed a 'refuse destructor and incinerator' because it was said to be cheaper than tipping.
- Jimmy Thomas of George Street, Pill, was elected MP for Derby.

Jimmy Thomas was a powerful influence in the National Union of Railwaymen and became its General Secretary and took the union through a few nationwide rail strikes. He became a labour MP for Derby in 1910. By 1929 his popularity had increased and he became Lord Privy Seal when Ramsay MacDonald was Prime Minister.

Later in his career in 1936 he was forced to resign when he was leaking the Budget secrets to his stockbroker son Leslie and others. At the end of his life he came back to Wales and lived in Porthcawl.

Commerce
- E.W. King & Son, joiners, moved to Newport from Cardiff to become an important industry in the town. They employed many carpenters.

People
- More bodies were discovered from the 1909 Docks disaster.
- Seven Newport rugby players picked for the Lions tour of South Africa.

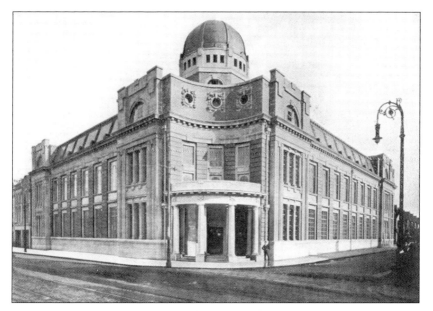

The Art College at Clarence Place was opened as a Technical College in 1910. It became an Art College in 1966. Cost of the original building £41,000.

The Corn Exchange Tower in High St was built in 1878, the architect was Benjamin Lawrence, and it was remodelled in 1910. It was demolished in 1970s. The Corn Exchange which was a business building where corn dealers bought and sold their corn it was rented from Lord Tredegar.

- Johnny Basham (b. 1890) had successful fights and became a celebrity in Newport. He became Middleweight champion of Europe and Welterweight champion of Britain and won a Lonsdale belt outright. Johnny Basham was a very generous man and a soft touch for any 'scrounger' and lost a lot of money that way to others. He died a poor man at the age of 57 in 1947 in 12 Mountjoy Place. His Lonsdale belt was eventually sold by his widow in Christie's London in 1954.

His first professional fights were in 1910 but began disastrously as he was knocked out in both of his first two contests. He improved after this. He served in the war and had it not been for this he could have become World Champion.

After a fight in 1913 with Harry Price, Johnny was arrested because Price died. He was released a short time afterwards.

Johnny is buried in St Woolos Cemetery.

- Presentation of medals to eight heroes of the Docks disaster of 1909 by HRH Duke of Connaught (medals to James Andrews, Charles Crogan, Anthony Kinsella, William Williams, George Bradford, John Aldridge, Daniel McCarthy, George Osbourne.

Places and Events
- A public baths was built in Pill near the Police station close to the dock entrance.
- The Waterloo Hotel was opened close to the main entrance to the docks.

Waterloo Hotel at the corner opposite the docks main entrance 2007. It was built by William Moore and catered for ship's captains and other senior officers. In the early 1900s bed and breakfast cost 5s. 6d.
Over the years its clock tower needed repair and in 2007 it was restored to its full glory and opened as a Hotel and Bistro. The external restoration has made it look almost as it was 100 years ago.

- The Art College at Clarence Place was opened as a Technical College.
- The 'Plaza Cinema' (also called the Tivoli and by some the 'Bug House') opened at Commercial Road, Pill. It closed in 1957. It was well-known for 'its penny rush' on a Saturday morning when queues of eager children paid their penny and then rushed in to get the best seats for the film. It was owned by a Mr Averbuck, his name always amused people. (People often thought his name was 'have a bug' as often children returned home with such.)
- The Corn Exchange building was remodelled. It was demolished in the 1970s.
- Clarence Place about 1910 was the location where Caerleon Road, Chepstow Road and Corporation Road converged and led into town.

1911

The British and Worldwide Scene, Events and People

- The Coronation of King George V and Queen Mary was on 22nd January.
- Census showed England and Wales with 36 million people, Scotland 4.6 and Northern Ireland 1.25 million.
- The Parliament Act removed the absolute veto of the House of Lords for any legislation but allowed a delaying process.
- Members of Parliament were paid for the first time.

- The ill-fated British liner *Titanic* was launched at the Harland & Wolff's shipyard in Belfast.

Sketch of the Titanic. She sank in 1912. Some 1,513 people died out of the 2,220 people on board

- The first ever Indianapolis 500 motor car race was run in USA and won by Ray Harroun.

A sketch of the car No. 32 the bright yellow Marmon Wasp which Ray Harroun won the first Indianapolis 500 at an average speed of 74.50 mph. The 500 miles took him 6 hours 42 mins.

- Sir William Gilbert died. He was an English writer of comic opera in conjunction with Sir Arthur Sullivan.
- The National Insurance was introduced in Britain by Chancellor Lloyd George, Liberal statesman. It provided insurance for workers against ill health and unemployment. Ill health was granted 10s. per week and unemployment 7s. per week. Maternity benefits were 30s. per week
- The siege of Sidney Street, East London, took place when anarchists were besieged by police and soldiers. A group of Latvians anarchists tried to rob a jeweller's shop by tunnelling into it. The plot was discovered and an unarmed policeman was shot. Most of the gang escaped but days later were found in Sidney Street which was besieged. The leader 'Peter the Painter' was never found. It attracted so much attention that the Home Secretary, Winston Churchill was present to give advice.
- Ronald Amundsen (1872-1928) the Norwegian explorer became the first to reach the South Pole, 35 days ahead of Captain Scott who reached the Pole on 17th January. Amundsen was later killed in 1928 in a plane crash over the Arctic Ocean.
- The first Monte Carlo car rally was instigated by Prince Albert 1st in Monaco and was won by Henri Rougier in a Turcat-Mery. Rougier was also a pioneering aviator.

The Local Scene, Events and People

Civic and Political

- Mayor was John McGinn. He was born in Omagh, Northern Ireland in 1862. He studied medicine in Scotland and came to Newport in 1890 as a doctor.
- Population of Newport was 83,691 with 14,249 dwellings.

Commerce

- Seamen's strike.
- Railway strike brings out troops in East Newport to quell the trouble.

People

- Captain Charles Gower was made Chief Constable of Newport.

Places and Events

- Municipal Secondary school or Higher Elementary School built on Stow Hill; it was opened 7th July, 1911 and this in later years became part of St Julian's High School and latterly Queen's High School before that closed.

Municipal Secondary School, Stow Hill alfter it became St Julian's High School. The building remained and became Stow Hill Secondary Modern School and then this merged to become the lower school of Newport High School, Queen's Hill. The new St Julian's High School was opened in 1940.

- The Congregational Chapel, Dock Street, purchased by St Paul's Church and re-named St James Church. Cost £1,400.
- St Barnabas Church, New Ruperra Street, Pill closed and the congregation transferred to other churches.

Youth group thought to be naval cadets outside St Paul's Church.

Jimmy Thomas MP went to the National School. He worked in the chemist shop close by before joining the Great Western Railway Company as a cleaner. The King William Public House is on the corner plot on right.

The crossroads of Commercial Road and Cardiff Road with the Salutation Inn prominent.

1912

The British and Worldwide Scene, Events and People

- Captain Robert Scott 1868-1912, perished in the snows of Antarctica while on his 800 mile return journey across the snow from his successful expedition to reach the South Pole. One of the party, Lawrence Oates, made the now famous comment, 'I am going outside and I may be some time', he never returned. They all died towards the end of March only 11 miles from their next supply base.
- The 'unsinkable' White Star passenger liner *Titanic* sank during her maiden voyage from Southampton to New York by hitting an iceberg off Newfoundland (15th April).
- The Royal Flying Corps was founded, later to be known as the RAF.
- William Booth (1820-1912) died at the age of 83. He was an English social reformer, evangelist and founder of the Salvation Army. He was born in Nottingham, the son of a builder.
- Coal miners' strike in Britain.
- The newspaper the *Daily Herald* was started; it stopped production in 1964.
- Discovery of the 'missing link' skull called the 'Piltdown Man'. This was revealed to be a hoax in 1953. The forgers were unknown.
- Outbreak of the first Balkans War which was a contributory factor in starting World War I.
- Former USA President Theodore Roosevelt (1858-1919), 26th President (1901-1909) and the youngest at 42, was shot and seriously wounded by a demented man in Milwaukee. Roosevelt won the Nobel Peace Prize for his part in ending the Russian/Japanese War in 1905.
- Woodrow Wilson elected the first Democratic President of USA for 20 years.
- Fifth Olympics opened in Stockholm.

The Local Scene, Events and People

Civic and Political
- Mayor was C.P. Simmonds. He was a well respected church worker and businessman of the Maindee area owning a few grocery shops.
- Newport Fire Brigade bought its first motor fire engine, replacing the horse-drawn equipment.
- Enlarged Museum & Art Gallery opened in Dock Street. The original building opened in 1895.

Commerce
- Newport & Mon County Association Football Club team was founded by a group of local businessmen; later it was called Newport County AFC.
- John Cashmore Ltd start a shipbreakers yard in Newport and acquire many famous liners and battleships over the years, until it closed in the late 1970s.
- Much of the land in Newport belonged to Lord Tredegar. He generously donated land to hospitals, churches and other good causes, charging minimal rents.

People
- Newport rugby team defeated the South African touring team 9-3.

Places and Events
- Golf became popular amongst the 'upper class'. Since 1900 it had been established at 'The Great Oak' Rogerstone when the new course was opened.
- Talking films become available in cinema.
- The Wrenford Hall built at St Paul's Church Commercial Street at a cost of £1,300 and named after a former vicar. It was used by the Sea Cadets and was demolished in 2002.
- Annual Conference of the Trade Union Congress was held in Newport.
- The foundation stone of the Monmouthshire Training College, Caerleon laid. When built it was set on fire by Miss Margaret Haig Thomas because it only admitted males. In 1883 she married Sir Humphrey Mackworth and after her father's death (Viscount David Alfred Thomas), she became Viscountess Mackworth and Lady Rhondda.
- The National School (previously the Poor House) opposite St Paul's Church in Commercial Street was demolished.

- South Dock was extended making the docks complex one of the biggest in the world.

Water let into South Dock. It was originally opened in 1893 but was extended and became the largest dock in the world in 1914 when it opened for shipping.

Health
- Dr Garrod Thomas (1853-1931), a generous benefactor to the Royal Gwent Hospital, and a local Councillor and highly respected citizen of Newport, was knighted. His house is now the Newport Mansion House, used by the mayor.

Dr Garrod Thomas lived at 4 Stow Park Circle , the house now owned by Newport as the 'Mansion House'.

1913

The British and Worldwide Scene, Events and People

- The bodies of the Antarctic explorers who reached the South Pole in 1912 were discovered on 19th February (Captain Scott, Oates, Evans, Wilson and Bowers).
- The Trade Union Act in Britain gave the unions the right to use their funds for political work.
- The first Chelsea Flower show opened in London.

- Charlie Chaplin made his debut in the silent film 'Making a Living'.

  Sir Charles Spencer Chaplin (1889-1977), was an English motion-picture actor. He first achieved worldwide fame through his performances in silent films. He was one of the most creative artists in film history. Went on to be a film director and producer.

- Richard Nixon was born (1913-1994). He became the 37th president in 1968 to 1974 when he resigned over the 'Watergate' scandal of 'bugging' meetings of his opponents.
- The zip fastener as we know it today was patented by a Swedish engineer named Gideon Sunback, from New Jersey, USA.
- The Mona Lisa painting by Leonardo Da Vinci was recovered (it was stolen in 1912).
- The first crossword puzzle was published in a weekend supplement of the *New York World* and compiled by Liverpool-born Arthur Wynne.

The Local Scene, Events and People

Civic and Political
- Mayor was Dr John Lloyd Davies and made an Alderman in 1923 and a Freeman of the town in 1936.

- Godfrey Charles Morgan, Viscount Tredegar, died and was buried at St Basil's Church Bassaleg. He never married, therefore the title Viscount was passed to Courtney Morgan, the son of his brother Frederick of Ruperra.

Funeral of Godfrey Charles Morgan on the way to St Basil's Church, Bassaleg.

- Monument to Viscount Tredegar in Newport town centre.

Lord Tredegar was one of the most influential and generous benefactors to Newport who gained his wealth from owing ground rents and income from the coal industry. His statue was placed in the present position in 1992 and a time capsule was placed in the plinth of the monument.
It was previously located in Park Square in a park known to locals as either 'The old people's park' or 'the Old Man's Park'. It was reputed that at midnight he would get off the monument and walk around Newport.

- The use of motor omnibuses as a means of transport on Newport streets was refused by the council.
- Britain's worst mining disaster took place at the colliery in Senghenydd, Glamorgan; 436 miners were killed.

Commerce
- Coal exports accounted for 90 per cent of Newport Docks trade.
- Newport General Post Office, High St was extended.

People
- Suffragette Margaret Mackworth was sent to prison by Newport Magistrates. She later became Lady Rhondda.
- Houdini, the great escapologist, jumped from Newport Bridge and made an underwater escape from a sack in which he was tied up and chained. He did so unharmed.
- Newport boxer Johnny Basham knocked out Harry Price of Liverpool, who later died. Basham was arrested but subsequently released. Basham was a sergeant in the Royal Welsh Fusiliers during World War I. He won the British Welterweight title and the Lonsdale belt in 1914.

Places and Events
- A drinking fountain was presented to the town by the women from the Temperance Association and was placed outside the main entrance to Belle Vue Park, Friars Road (cost £50). In 1996 this was transferred to near the entrance to St Woolos Church.

The water drinking fountain presented to the town by the women from the Temperance Association. It was hoped that it would encourage people to drink water rather than alcoholic drinks which were seen to be ruining home life and society. In 1996 this was transferred to near the entrance to St Woolos Church, Stow Hill.

- The Gem Cinema at the junction of Commercial Road and Capel Street, Pill, opened (also commonly known as 'The Flea Pit' or 'The Laugh and Scratch'; closed in 1954). During the early days the manager, Mr Gill, would stand in his black dinner jacket and white gloves outside directing the scruffy children into the cinema and sometimes having to keep order as the film got to the exciting bits. He often had to manhandle children and throw them out or stop kids trying to crawl in with the crowd without paying. He did this with much dignity.
- The Coliseum Cinema opened in Clarence Place (closed in 1987).

- Monmouthshire County Training College for Schoolmasters, Caerleon, was opened.

The teacher training college in 1914. While it was being built it was attacked and burned by suffragettes because only males were admitted.

Health

- King George V gave official approval to change the name of 'The Newport and Monmouthshire Hospital' to 'The Royal Gwent Hospital'.
- The Friars House, Friars Road, with its 14 acres of land was given to The Royal Gwent Hospital by Rt Hon. Courtney Morgan, Lord Tredegar.

The Friars House and the surrounding land was given to the Hospital by Lord Tredegar as a memorial to his late uncle. There is some evidence that the original building was the monastery of the White Friars of the Carmelite order then became the home of various families from the 16th century and eventually rebuilt in late 19th century when the owner was Octavius Morgan (brother of Lord Tredegar). It was eventually given to the Hospital in 1913.

1914

The British and Worldwide Scene, Events and People

- The intense nationalism and rivalry existing throughout Europe for many years of the 19th and early 20th century was a precursor for World War I. The relatively local war between Austria-Hungary and Serbia occurred in July 1914 caused by the assassination of Archduke Francis Ferdinand, heir to the Austrian-Hungarian thrones, on 28th June by a Serb nationalist. It escalated into a World War involving 32 nations: 28 were aligned with Britain, France, Russia, Italy and later USA and called the Allies and four were aligned with Germany, Austria-Hungary, Turkey and Bulgaria. Many nations in Europe had been building up defensive armaments and armies and navies prior to the outbreak of war. The growth of the build-up of armaments was financially crippling nations and two major conferences were held to consider worldwide disarmament (1899 and 1907) with little success.
- Germany invaded Belgium on 4th August.
- Britain declared war on the German group on 4th August and Japan joined on Britain's side on 23rd August. USA waited until April 1917 before entering the war.
- Japan declared war on Germany and Germany upon Russia in August.
- The first British troops land in France on 16th August.
- The battle of Mons in Belgium on the French border took place. This was the first major engagement fought by Britain against Germany.
- The first German Zeppelin (airship) appeared over the British coast.
- First air raid on British soil took place and a single bomb fell on a the grounds of St James rectory in Dover.
- The Panama Canal opened. The official and publicized first ship to make the voyage was the *Ancon* on 15th August, 1914. It took over 30 years from the initial effort in 1880 to actually open the canal in 1914.
- The battle at Ypres (Belgium), May 1915, was the beginning of trench warfare on the Western Front. Ypres, like many battlefields in the area of that town, was the location of a few battles of to and fro movements of the Allies and the German forces. Hundreds of soldiers on both sides died in the battles and many died from injuries becoming infectious in the muddy, dirty and unhygienic trenches. Chlorine gas was also used by the Germans. This contravened the 1907 Hague convention of methods of warfare but it was not long before Britain followed suit. Ypres was called 'the gas hell'.
- It was estimated that 91,000 died because of gasses of various sorts and related injuries and 1.2 million were hospitalized at some time as a result of gas attacks.
- Soldiers often grouped in a huddle to keep warm and sheltering in a shell hole to keep out of the biting winds and snow. In some areas trenches and underground tunnels protected them from the elements and gunfire.
- Britain's first police women went on duty in Grantham in Lincolnshire.
- Cyprus was annexed to Britain and later in 1925 became a Crown colony and became independent of Britain in 1959.

- A sister ship to the *Titanic*, the *Britannic* was built and was going to be 'superior' to it in all aspects but it also ended up at the bottom of the sea, the Aegean Sea, as a result of a mine laid by German U-boats in 1916. Its captain was Charles Bartlett. The *Britannic* made its maiden voyage in 1915 and was used as a hospital ship during its short life.
- Cub Scouts were founded in England.
- Sir William Alexander Smith founder of the Boy's Brigade died.
- The bra was patented in America by Mary Phelps Jacob.
- The polio vaccine pioneer, Jonas Salk was born in New York, he died in 1995. The polio vaccine was developed in 1952 and implemented in 1954. Within 10 years it reduced the incidence of polio by 95 per cent.
- George Eastman announced the invention of a process of colour photography. It was later marketed by Eastman Kodak.
- The Welsh poet Dylan Thomas was born in Swansea on 27th October, he died in New York 1953. His famous book about the inhabitants of the mythical village of Llareggub (read this backwards) was published in 1954. Dylan Thomas wrote a short poem on the death of his father which starts:

> Do not go gentle into that good night,
> Old age should burn and rave at close of day
> Rage, rage against the dying of the light

The story is called *Under Milkwood* and is a well-known commentary on a mythical but realistic Welsh village. Some of the characters include: Captain Cat - 'The old blind sea captain who dreams of his deceased sea friends'; Myfanwy Price - 'The dressmaker and sweet shop owner who dreams of Mog Edwards and marriage'; Mr Pugh - 'School master, dreams of murdering his wife'; Mr & Mrs Floyd - 'The cocklers, an elderly couple who appear to be the only couple to sleep peacefully in the village'; Mrs Ogmore-Pritchard - 'The innkeeper who must have everything clean'. Thomas wrote in a hut close to Langharne Castle.

Langharne Castle

The Local Scene, Events and People

Civic and Political
- The Mayor at the outbreak of war was Frederick Pring Robjent.
- First World War I deaths and casualties occurred. Many were members of Newport Athletic Club who were amongst the first to join up. A list of their names is on the gates of the Athletic ground.
- The Council purchased The Somerton Estate for £21,815.
- The town was 'darkened' at night for fear of Zeppelin raids and bombings.
- The German liner *Belgia* was captured by Newport Police outside the Alexandra docks on 4th August. The German reservists on board were taken into custody. Captain Cutliffe, who was in charge of the operation, died in 1950. SS *Belgia* had 76 German reservists on board.

SS Belgia.

Commerce
- The Uskside Engineering Works in Church Street, Pill, made a major contribution to the war effort by producing a large amount of armament. Much female labour was used.
- Great Western Railway fitting workshop in Maesglas converted to manufacture shells and other wartime material.
- Whitehead Iron & Steel Co. Ltd plan move from Tredegar to a 12 acre site at Mendalgief Road, Pill. Housing for many families that moved were created in Pill and the Gaer.

Police in the photograph are, standing; Constables E.H .Dean, H. Birch, G.E. Nelmes, S. Cullimore, I Bailey, D.C. Bowen, A.H. Herbert; seated, E. Caldicott, Sergt T. Davies, Capt. G.E. Gower (Chief Constable), Inspector S. Cox, Sergt F. Drewett and Constable A. Homer.

People
- Birching for petty crime was common.
- Alexander Graber, better known as Alexander Cordell, was born in Ceylon (now Sri Lanka) and died in 1997. He became a famous author who did most of his research in Newport Reference Library. He wrote *Rape of the Fair Country* which tells the story of a family as it struggles through a time of poverty. It was set in Blaenavon during the time of coal mining and steel making. He wrote other books based on the times of industrial Wales of the 1800s. There is an inn named after him near Govilon, Abergavenny.

Places and Events
- Final phase of Alexandra Dock opened by Prince Arthur.

HRH Prince Arthur visiting the opening of new docks in Newport.

- The 'Electric Theatre' at the junction of High Street and Station Approach was up for auction and was bought as an extension to the adjoining Post Office.

Health
- Beechwood House in Beechwood Park used as a Hospital.
- Cefn Mably House was opened as a nursing home.
- First casualties from the war were admitted to hospital wards in 'The Friars', Friars Road, close to the top entrance of Belle Vue Park.
- During the 1914-18 period almost 800 servicemen were admitted to the Royal Gwent Hospital with injuries and a wide range of diseases.
- The first soldiers admitted to the Royal Gwent Hospital were Belgians. Wounded soldiers admitted to hospital wore distinctive blue uniforms and were nicknamed the 'Blue Boys'. Many local people were kind to these soldiers when convalescing and visited them and also entertained them in their homes.
- The 'Workhouse' on Stow Hill also took in wounded soldiers and became a temporary military hospital manned by the Royal Army Medical Corps and the nurses came from the Queen Alexandra's Imperial Nursing Service.
- The first blood transfusion took place in a Brussels hospital; it would not be long for the technique to reach Newport hospitals also.

1915

The British and Worldwide Scene, Events and People

- Germans and British begin to use poisonous gas in warfare.
- German submarines try to blockade Britain to prevent import of food and arms.
- Cunard passenger liner *Lusitania* torpedoed by a German submarine on 7th May with the loss of 1,198 lives. It was torpedoed off southern Ireland when on its way from America, sinking in 20 minutes. A few Newport people who survived were Viscount A.F. Thomas of Llanwern and his daughter Margaret.
- The Zeppelin or airships were developed in 1914 in Germany and could reach a maximum speed of 136 kph and reach a height of 4,250 metres. The Zeppelin had five machine-guns and could carry a load of 4,400 lb. of bombs. In January 1915, two Zeppelins, each 190 metres long, flew over the east coast of England and bombed Great Yarmouth and King's Lynn. The first Zeppelin raid on London took place on 31st May, 1915. The raid killed 28 people and injured 60 more.
- British fighter pilots and anti-aircraft gunners became very good at bringing down Zeppelins and over 70 were shot down over Britain. Many places had Zeppelin raids including, Sunderland, Edinburgh and the Midlands. By the end of 1916 at least 550 UK civilians had been killed by German Zeppelin attacks.
- Edith Cavell, English nurse, executed by a German firing squad in Brussels for helping Allied prisoners to escape over the Dutch border. She was matron of a Red Cross Hospital in Brussels.
- The German Junkers 'J1', which was the first all-metal aeroplane, flew at Dessau.
- British troops in France were issued for the first time with hand grenades.
- Tanks first appeared in warfare.
- The Allies began a retreat from the disastrous Dardanelles campaign.
- W.G. Grace (1848-1915), who was a legendary English cricketer, died in Eltham, Kent. The skills of W.G. Grace were extraordinary and he contributed to making cricket the popular game it is today.

The drawing was done by a local Newport young school girl at the time, Edna M. Vaughan, who was aware of the horrors of war as neighbours, friends and local families had all experienced the loss of loved ones and seen the injuries of many soldiers including physically wounded, mentally scarred and blinded soldiers. The picture had a poem attached to it that read:

'Hers the comfort, hers the conquest, hers the flag of life
unfurled
Hers the sorrow, hers the suffering, hers the love that
rules the world'

- The Woman's Institute organisation was founded in Britain in Anglesey, Wales. It was originally started in Canada in 1897.
- Passport photographs were first required by British citizens.
- Railway disaster occurred near Gretna Green, killing 227 people, mostly soldiers on their way to Gallipoli. This was, and still is, the worst train accident in Britain.

The Local Scene, Events and People

Civic and Political
- The Mayor was Charles Thomas JP.
- The *South Wales Argus* Smokers' Fund provided British servicemen with 35 cigarettes, 2 oz. tobacco and a packet of matches for every 6*d.* donated.
- New Newport Bridge was being constructed over the Usk in the centre of the town.

Places and Events
- 'Coed Melyn Park', Risca Road was opened. Commonly called 'The Jews Wood'.
- 16 Charles Street used as Elementary Education Offices and School Medical Department.
- Shaftesbury Café on Newport Bridge becomes Jays furniture shop.
- Band concerts common in Belle Vue Park.
- Last commercial barge to pass along the Moderator Wharf.

Canal barges come close to the river wharfs to unload cargo.

Last barge to unload at the Moderator wharf at a site that is probably now Kingsway.

Health
- St Woolos Church was being restored and dedicated.
- Beechwood House in the park was used as a tuberculosis hospital for servicemen.
- Royal Gwent Hospital was in gross financial difficulties and a house-to-house collection helped alleviate the problem.
- Medical and ambulance brigade crews were recruited for war duties.

1916

The British and Worldwide Scene, Events and People

- The Easter Rebellion took place in Dublin against British rule; this was followed by reprisals by the British troops called the 'Black and Tans'.
- Daylight Saving Time, advocated by William Willett, was introduced in Britain. Willett had been vigorously campaigning for 'daylight saving' since 1907 until his death in 1915, from influenza. Willett was a builder of high repute, examples of Willett Building Services town houses are to be seen in areas such as Chelsea and Hove. William Willett is the great-great-grandfather of Chris Martin, singer/songwriter from the band Coldplay.
- Lloyd George becomes British Prime Minister of a coalition government.

War Matters
- The final withdrawal of Allied troops from Gallipoli took place after an unsuccessful expedition to capture Constantinople (now called Istanbul).
- Military conscription was introduced in Britain.
- Battle of Verdun took place from February to December and there were appalling losses of life on both sides.
- Zeppelins bombed Paris for the first time.
- Military tanks were first used by the British Army in the Somme offensive which ended on 13th November with British losses of 42,000 with 20,000 dead on the first day. There were over one million casualties.
- Battle of Jutland where the British and German fleets conducted the only major face to face battle of the fleets during the war.
- National Savings Certificates went on sale in Britain.
- Lord Kitchener (1850-1916), the famous British soldier and leader was drowned on 5th June when his ship HMS *Hampshire en route* to Russia was sunk by a mine put down by the German U-boat U75. 643 men died of drowning or exposure.

The Local Scene, Events and People

Civic and Political
- The Mayor was Alfred Swash.
- Councillor Peter Wright persuades the council to provide meals for poor children.

Commerce
- Mannesman Metal Tube Works (later Stewart & Lloyd) was opened in Newport.
- Braithwaite Iron & Steel Co. comes to Cork Wharf, Alexandra Dock, moving from West Bromwich. This was welcomed as it created opportunities for employment.

People
- Johnny Morris, the famous broadcaster of animal and children's stories, was born.
- Twelve conductresses employed on the trams to replace the men going to war.
- Johnny Basham won the Lonsdale Belt outright.

Places and Events
- Second railway tunnel under Stow Hill was completed.

Health
- Sir John Beynon gave his mansion at the Coldra to the Health Authority for use as a maternity hospital in memory of his mother Lady Lydia Beynon.

The Lydia Beynon Maternity Hospital was later sold and became a small Hotel. It was developed in the twentieth century by the millionaire Terry Matthews who converted it into the Celtic Manor Hotel and Resort containing world class golf courses and tennis courts.

- Royal Gwent Hospital extended to include new operating theatres, additional wards and a casualty department.
- Hospitals had a number of war-wounded soldiers to treat and care for.

1917

The British and Worldwide Scene, Events and People

- The British Royal family adopted the name of 'House of Windsor' in place of 'House of Saxe-Corburg-Gotha'.
- Balfour declared that Britain would support a Jewish State in Palestine on 2nd November and on 9th December British forces captured Jerusalem.
- Dame Vera Lynn, the English vocalist and called the 'Forces Sweetheart' during World War II, was born in London as Vera Welch.
- The Women's Army Auxiliary Corps was formed.
- Sir Arthur Lee donated 'Chequers' to the Nation as a country home for the British Prime Ministers (handed over in 1921). Its history dates back to 11th century and the present house has had many famous guests both recent and distant (e.g. Lady Jane Grey the Queen for nine days) in the time just after Henry VIII.
- Canadian troops successfully take Vimy Ridge in France (9-12th April) as a result of clever war tactics. The ridge had been held by German troops who repelled many attempts to clear them out. It was estimated that 200,000 lives, 10,600 of these being Canadians, had been lost trying to take the ridge. These figures seem almost unbelievable today. This battle was said to be the turning point in the war in that area.

- USA declared war on Germany (17th April).
- The Bolshevik Revolution of 1917 overthrew the Czarist rule and Prime Minister Alexander Kerensky's government. Lenin (1870-1924) soon became the ruler in the state which was declared to be a Republic on 15th September and called USSR.
- Tzar Nicholas of Russia abdicates.
- John F. Kennedy (1917-1963), the American Democratic statesman and 35th President, was born on 29th May in Massachusetts, the second of nine children. He was assassinated on 22nd November, 1963 at 12.30 pm in Dallas, Texas by Lee Harvey Oswald a former US marine, who was himself assassinated two days later by Jack Ruby.
- Indira Gandhi (née Nehru) (1917-1984), the Indian stateswoman and first woman president, was born in Allanabad. Indira Gandhi was assassinated in 1984 by a Sikh member of her own security guards.
- Mata Hari, who it was said danced nude on occasions, for the benefit of German officers, was shot by the Germans having been found guilty of espionage in Paris during the war. Some thought she was more of a showgirl than a spy.

The Local Scene, Events and People

Civic and Political
- The Mayor was William Evans.
- Many events organized by churches, works and concerts etc. to raise funds for families of soldiers and sailors killed in the war.

Commerce
- Lovells Athletic AFC soccer team was formed and proved to be a successful side, even winning the Welsh Cup.

A Lovells team of the 1920s. Lovells Athletic AFC was formed in 1917/18 and disbanded in 1969. They once won the Welsh cup. Lovells Sweets, which sponsored the team, was a flourishing confectionery firm. Their toffee and 'Minto' were well known. Some famous players who once played for Lovells include Harry Clarke (Tottenham and England), and Bill Shankly, the famous manager of Liverpool. Lovells was also called Rexville at some time.

People
- More women bus drivers, as well as conductresses, were employed by the council in Newport.

Places and Events
- The peacocks were moved from Beechwood Park to Belle Vue Park.

Health
- Food shortages caused concern for good health, often queues for food.

Distribution of hot pots on Christmas morning 1914. William Blow the Chairman of the Newport Christmas Hot Pot Fund is in the centre of the picture.

- Many people tried, in various ways, to help the poor and needy. One lady interviewed said she and her neighbours collected the stale bread (in those days it did not last long) and took it to one family with six children for them to make bread pudding.

Events
- Electric tram service to the Docks entrance on Alexandra Rd was started.
- First covered double-decker trams were used.

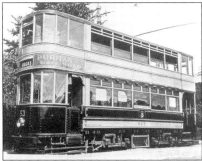

An open top tram. The poor driver and upper level passengers got wet when it rained.

A closed top tram (what an innovation!) on the Chepstow Road-Docks route.

1918

The British and Worldwide Scene, Events and People

- The Armistice for the end of World War I was signed in Admiral Foch's railway coach in Compiegne, France. Armistice Day commemorates this event at 11 am on 11th November each year ever since.

Newport, like all other British towns wanted to thank the forces who fought for the country and to remember those who gave their lives. Processions and street parties were the orders of the day.

- H.A.L. Fisher's Education Act of Parliament raised the school leaving age to 14. This was seen to be a revolution for the advance of education. He planned to extend tertiary education also, even with part time university education, to allow more people to be educated to a higher level. This he was not able to implement. He died in 1940.
- National Savings stamps went on sale in Britain.
- Recruitment started for the Women's Royal Naval Service in Britain.
- Women over 30 were first permitted to vote in elections to the Parliament at Westminster and allowed to be candidates in the General Election to the House of Commons.
- The British newspaper the *Sunday Express* began publication.
- The German fleet mutinied in Kiel.
- Spanish flu epidemic when it arrived in Britain was said to have killed twice as many people as died in World War I.
- Billy Graham, the American Evangelist, was born in North Carolina.
- Woodrow Wilson went to France, becoming the first American President to visit a foreign country.

The Local Scene, Events and People

Civic and Political
- Mayor was Henry Charles Parfitt.
- Member of Parliament was Lewis Haslam (Labour).
- Rationing introduced because of the scarcity of certain foodstuffs caused by the war, but only lasted 12 months.
- Councillor Peter Wright advocated building more council houses, Newport needing at least 100 extra. He said, 'living in apartments, as hundreds of families do, is little better than living in hell'. He met with a lot of opposition on the council.

Commerce
- Transport Employees Institute and Canteen opened on the third floor of the Old Tramways Stables and Depot, Clarence Place. The Odeon Cinema was later built on the site.
- A house in David Street was sold for £125. Letting value 8s. 6d. per week.
- Newport Dockers raised over £6,000 to help wives and children of comrades who had joined the forces at wartime and many were killed or 'lost in action'.

People
- Many Newport soldiers and sailors killed in the war and those returning often were scarred with shell shock or nightmares for years to come. Some suffered from the effects of chlorine gas and others were blinded, many lost limbs.
- With returning soldiers there was a job crisis as many women had been used to working and doing a man's job when they were in the war. Employers were put in a difficult position over employment.
- Billy Lucas, Welsh International soccer player and once manager of Newport County AFC 1953-74, was born.

Health
- Royal Gwent Hospital had a debt of £3,000 but it was wiped out by gifts from individuals and by Newport industrialists.
- Many concerts and collections made for war widows and children and also in aid of the Royal Gwent Hospital.
- After the Armistice in 1918, the directors of the Royal Gwent Hospital decided in future years to use the land around the hospital for a fund raising Fete each August Bank Holiday, starting 1919. This became a well known event of the town and was accompanied by a Carnival and procession. It also held a 'Charity Ball' to raise funds. A ticket in the 1940s cost the expensive amount of 17s. 6d.
- There was evidence that 'Ye Olde English Fayre' was held as early as 1882 in aid of the Newport Infirmary and Dispensary on Stow Hill. The Fayre was held at the Albert Hall. Small Fetes were held periodically and records show some in 1906 raised £80.

1919

The British and Worldwide Scene, Events and People

- The mighty German High Seas fleet was handed over to the British fleet for internment at Scapa Flow in the Orkneys and then scuttled on 19th June.
- Viscountess Nancy Astor MP became the first woman member of Parliament to take her seat in the House of Commons.
- The Nazi party was founded by Anton Drexler in Munich, Germany.
- The Fascist party was founded by Mussolini in Italy.
- Frank Winfield(1879-1919) died. He was the founder of F.W. Woolworth's shops.
- A massive meteor landed in Lake Michigan, USA.
- Pierre Auguste Renoir the French painter died.

The Local Scene, Events and People

Civic and Political

- The Mayor was Peter Wright who was a famous sportsman and renowned wrestler.

Peter Wright was a very popular person in Newport because of the way he fought on behalf of the poorer people of Newport and wanted a better standard of living and better housing. He became the first Labour Alderman in 1928. He was a competitive and high class sportsman and an equally ardent worker for the socialist cause. This photograph shows him with the St Michael's Gym Class in the early 1900s.

Peter Wright

- The Borough Architect warns that houses in Pill were suspect because the land on which they were built was filled by imported ballast from ships.
- The Transporter Bridge shows losses of £76,000 since it opened in 1906. It was called 'The White Elephant'.
- Newport citizens take part in the Rat Week for the extermination of rats in the town. Three pence was offered for each rat tail taken to a police station. Over 1,000 rats were trapped or killed.
- Race riots in George Street between black and white people quelled by police. Considerable damage to property, 34 people arrested.

Commerce
- Whitehead Iron & Steel Co. build a factory at Mendelgief Rd, Pill.
- It was revealed that secret construction work was undertaken during the war at Alexandra Docks.

People
- Der Chong, the keeper of the Chinese Laundry in Commercial Road, was fined for using his premises for the smoking of opium.
- Arthur Gould, the legendary Newport Rugby player died.

Boys Brigade was a popular organization. The groups had a wide range of activities and a strong link to a local church. 'Church Parade' was a regular event.

Places and Events
- Newport County AFC was reformed after the war and elected to the First Division of the Southern League, later to become the Third Division of the National Football League.
- Newport River Warmers Association use the disused Pill Police station in Temple Street and became the Pill YMCA.
- German U-boat submarine 91 was on show in the Old Town Dock.

Health
- The Royal Gwent Hospital was given a coat of arms with the motto 'The Best Wealth is Health'.
- Families unable to find accommodation were housed in the workhouse (Woolaston House - later St Woolos Hospital after the military had handed it back to the Board of Guardians).
- Fete to raise funds for the Royal Gwent Hospital was held in Friars Fields for the first time. The fete was organized until 1947 and raised a total of £104,193. This field later became part of the Hospital complex of buildings. The procession of Carnival entrants for fancy dress, displays etc. was sometimes one mile long. Mascots were sold to the public also in aid of the Hospital Funds. The evening firework display was a very popular attraction.
- Churches held a 'Hospital Sunday' when collections were taken up for hospital funds.
- Women's sport was becoming popular with football, rugby and tennis being played.

Chapter Four

The Nineteen-Twenties

This period, of 1920 to 1929, like the previous decade, was characterised by poverty due to lack of work and financial opportunities among some groups of Newport people. But poverty did not mean loss of dignity and many households were kept clean and food provided on family tables using resourcefulness with the small amount of money available. The shortage of money led to many disputes between employers and employees. Pill was particularly affected and the frustrations often ended up with excessive drunkenness and violence within and outside the family homes. The police files of those times are scattered with reports of violence, family rows, and all too many suicides.

To help the poorer people the 'Newport Hot Pot' fund continued to be organized, it made hot food and food parcels available to such groups. For all the poverty the churches and Sunday schools were well filled and at Whitsuntide the 'March of Witness' through the town of Sunday School pupils often numbered 10,000 to 12,000.

The docks were suffering from lack of trade and this affected employment. The population of Newport was expanding and this meant new housing and the boundaries of the town were expanding.

The changing status of women in society was reflected in the rise of women in employment, politics and academia.

1920

The British and Worldwide Scene, Events and People

- Nancy Astor became the first woman to speak in Parliament. Her husband Lord Astor died in 1919 and she stood for Parliament as the Unionist Party candidate and was elected with a large majority and remained as an MP until 1945. She was a champion of women's rights. She was born in America in 1879.
- Degree courses were first made available for women to study in Oxford University (14th October).
- The right to vote was given to women in America.
- The 35 ft Cenotaph war memorial in Whitehall London was unveiled by King George V on 11th November and the 'unknown warrior' was buried in Westminster Abbey.
- Pope John Paul II was born in Poland, the son of a junior officer in the army. He became the Pope in 1978 and was the first non-Italian Pope since 1542.
- The 7th Olympic games were opened in Antwerp.
- The Hague became the permanent seat of the International Court of Justice.
- The League of Nations (1920-1946) came into being holding its first meeting with 42 countries represented in Geneva from which Germany, Austria and Turkey were excluded and also the United States was not represented.

- The Bolsheviks defeated the White Russians during the Civil War.
- Prohibition started in USA banning the manufacture and sale of alcoholic drinks.
- The Mars Bar was invented by Frank Mars in USA for common sale (although he and his wife made a prototype in 1911).

The Local Scene, Events and People

Civic and Political
- The Mayor was William Augustus Linton.
- Churchill visited the town.
- The *South Wales Weekly Argus* reporter Kyle Fletcher (historian and writer) said that the Mountjoy House in Pill (now gone) was once the residence of Lord Mountjoy the Irish Pacifist.
- After a long meeting the Education Committee decided on 17th March to 'upgrade the curriculum and extend the length of the courses' for secondary pupils.

The curriculum was increased from four to six years, if abilities warranted it. Up to then the curriculum was no more than a focus on the '3 Rs'. An entrance exam was held. Science was included in the secondary curriculum along with a foreign language. Laboratories had to be built in some schools as practical work was encouraged.

In Stow Hill secondary school the noise of the trams coming up the hill, often disturbed the flow of lessons. The headmaster was Dr D.W. Oats.

Girls at Stow Hill secondary school in a cookery class. The headmistress was Miss M.M. Hughes

Commerce

- Tram and railway workers went on strike. Troops were called in, in case of an uprising.
- Strike at Whiteheads held up production of steel.
- Santon Ltd, famous for its water heaters, set up in Bridge Street. It moved to Lloyd St, Lliswerry in 1950.

People

- Councillor Peter Wright was offered a CBE by the King but he refused it saying that he would prefer the goodwill of the people to a title.
- Peter Wright paid for the town's newsboys to have a 'knife and fork' meal at the Town Hall.
- 10,000 Sunday School pupils parade through the town on Whit Monday and went to Athletic grounds and sang Whitsun Hymns conducted by Mr W.H. Bryant.
- Revd D.H. Williams retired from being Pastor of Ebenezer Welsh Church after 40 years of service.
- Jerry Shea was picked on the right wing for Wales Rugby team and scored 16 of the 19 points. He received four caps between 1919 and 1920 as a brilliant centre. He turned professional and joined Wigan Rugby League side where he played for three seasons. He always travelled from Newport and lived at 88 Alma Street. He still continued with his boxing career and later in the year beat Ivor Powell of Tredegar. When he retired from boxing at the age of 33 (his final fight was against Johnny Basham, a close friend) he worked at Alexandra docks. He died at the age of 55, in 1947 leaving a wife Catherine and seven children. He was described as 'lovable, romantic, daring, adventurous, kind' and was held in great esteem in Pill and a street is named after him.

Places and Events

- Newport Intermediate School on Queen's Hill was renamed Newport High School.
- Temporary Newport Bridge over the river was bought from London.
- Between the 1920s and the 1960s the Olympia cinema was opened in Skinner Street on a site on which once stood Hope Chapel and W.A. Baker, engineering works.
- There was an acute shortage of housing in Newport so the council started building homes for 'the working classes' and temporary accommodation was found in Woolaston House (the workhouse).

Health

- Rabies was diagnosed in some animals and warnings were posted for the public to be aware of rabid dogs.
- Money was raised by the spectators of a rugby match between Newport Athletic Club and Pill Harriers for the Hospital Fund.
- In this year £2,000 was raised by the Hospital Fete from various sources. The hospital launched an appeal for £200,000 for extensions.

1921

The British and Worldwide Scene, Events and People

- Prince Philip, Duke of Edinburgh, was born on the Greek Island of Corfu.
- The Irish Free State was established and became independent from United Kingdom (6th December).
- Car tax discs to be displayed on windscreens were introduced in Britain.
- British Legion was founded in London by Earl Haigh. It became the Royal British Legion in 1971.
- The Navy, Army and Air Force Institute, now commonly known as NAAFI, was founded in Britain.
- The Labour party voted their intent to nationalise coal mines when in power at their party conference in Blackpool. This came about in the early post-World War II period, in 1946.
- Sinn Féin riots in Dublin during which the Customs House was burnt down (7th February).
- The first American beauty contest was held in Atlantic City.
- Caruso, the great Italian tenor died.
- Benito Mussolini became leader of the Italian Fascists and in 1922 Premier and Dictator of Italy. He was only 37 years old, a son of a blacksmith. He joined sides with Hitler in World War II. In the final days of the war Mussolini attempted an escape to Switzerland with his mistress Clara Petacci, but Italian partisans captured them and shot them on 28th April, 1945.

The Local Scene, Events and People

Civic and Political
- The Mayor was E. Ambrose Charles.
- Population of Newport 92,369.
- Newport declared the seat of a Bishop. St Woolos Church designated the Protestant Cathedral of the Monmouth Diocese. The Revd Charles Green was enthroned.
- Prince of Wales (later King Edward VIII) visits the town and travelled on the Transporter Bridge and toured the docks.

Commerce
- Commerce was at a low ebb and suffering from the lack of work and worldwide financial depression.

People
- Jerry Shea, famous Newport & Wales rugby player, turned professional for Wigan.
- Ken Jones, the famous Newport and Wales Rugby player in later years, was born in Blaenavon. He became one of the finest rugby wings Newport ever had. He won 44 Welsh caps and played 293 times for Newport and was

their captain twice. He was also an international sprinter and was for some time a PE teacher in Newport High School, Queen's Hill. Ken Jones died on 18th April, 2006.

- 30th April, 1921 Newport Rugby Club fielded a side containing all Internationals from all the four British countries.

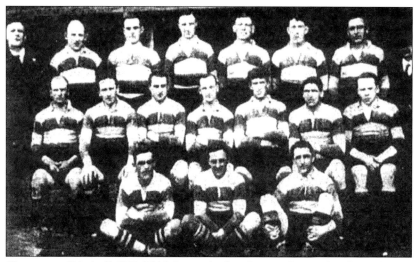

The team on 30th April, 1921, Welsh Internationals unless stated. Reg Edwards (England), I Attewell, H. Uzzell, R. Dibble (England), J. Whitfield, P. Jones, J. Wetter, E. Hammett (England), E. Birt, Reg Plummer, N. McPherson (Scotland), Jerry Shea, W.J. Roach (Ireland), Archie Brown, T.H. Vile, W.J. Martin.

Places and Events
- The Caerleon District war memorial was unveiled, later moving to another site as traffic increased in the streets.
- Newport Christian Hot Pot Fund distributed again at Christmas.
- Parish of St Julian's and Aaron was established which took its name from the two Christians who were martyred at Caerleon on 1st July, AD 303.
- Seventh Day Adventist Church was built on Chepstow Road.
- Motor bus service between Newport and Cardiff started.
- Morphine tablets discovered being smuggled in on a ship in the Alexandra Dock.

Health
- Sleeping sickness, tuberculosis and typhoid fever still caused concern in Newport.
- Black rats, common in the docks area, probably coming off the cargo ships arriving from abroad, fear that they carried the risk of bubonic plague.
- A new X-ray department was opened in Royal Gwent Hospital, also new skin and pathological departments.
- Paddle steamers were operating between Newport and Weston-super-Mare, etc.

Glen Avon *sailing up the Usk.*

1922

The British and Worldwide Scene, Events and People

- David Lloyd George resigns as Prime Minister in October after six years in office.
- Bonar Law (1858-1923) became Prime Minister of UK Parliament.
- The British Radio station '2LO' was established at Marconi House, The Strand, London and 'crystal set' radios became popular. BBC transmitted its first regional radio programme. Newport citizens welcome the introduction of the wireless as broadcasting begins. Many made their own simple radio receivers called 'Cat's Whiskers'.
- Radio licences were introduced in Britain at a cost of 10 shillings.
- The first ever British Legion Poppy Day appeal was held.
- The permanent Court of the International Justice held its first sitting at The Hague, Netherlands.
- Sir Ernest Shackleton, British Antarctic explorer, died when on an expedition off the coast of Western Australia.
- Dr Christian Barnard the South African, a pioneer surgeon of heart transplants in the 20th century, was born in Cape Province.
- The tomb of King Tutankhamen (1361-1352 BC) was discovered in Egypt by Lord Carnarvon. Tutankhamen was an Egyptian pharaoh of the 18th dynasty, the son-in-law of Akhenaton, whom he succeeded. He became pharaoh at the age of nine and ruled until his death at about the age of 18. He amassed a vast wealth some of which was buried with him and was discovered by Lord Carnarvon and Howard Carter in 1922.

- The Schutzstaffel (or SS), meaning 'protection squad' was formed in Germany. They became a severe and ruthless police force used by Hitler as a 'hit squad'.
- Heavy fighting in Dublin (2nd July) between the Irish (IRA) and Britain.
- Insulin was first discovered by the Canadian physiologists Sir Frederick Grant Banting and Charles Herbert Best and the British physiologist John James Rickard Macleod. It was used successfully in the treatment of diabetes. The molecular structure of insulin was the first protein structure to be worked out in 1955 by the British biochemist Frederick Sanger.

The Local Scene, Events and People

Civic and Political
- The Mayor was Edward Davies.
- Albert Augustus Newman resigns as Town Clerk. He was appointed in 1882 at the age of 22, then was the youngest Town Clerk to be appointed. He was made a Freeman of the Borough in 1922.
- Reginald Clarry (Conservative) became MP. He was knighted in 1936.

Commerce
- Many old war ships brought to Cashmore's in Pill for breaking up.
- Alexandra Docks very busy exporting coal. Estimated that six million tons a year were exported.
- Pill was the centre of commerce and industry and there were many small shops in the area. Other areas of the town were developing shops and industries as population and commerce increased.
- Whitehead's Rolling Mills starts operating at Courtybella Works, Mendalgief Road.
- Stow Hill Baths extended. Mixed bathing was not permitted and separate times were designated for male and female swimmers.

Stow Hill swimming baths had two 25 yard pools in its heyday. One pool, the new one, cost a few pence more than the other. Changing cubicles were all around the pools. In the 1940s the cost was 3d. and 6d. for the B or A pools. Children would often pay for the cheapest pool and then try to smuggle their way through the partition curtain to the more superior pool. When caught a 'whip' on the bottom by the attendant with a towel was a suitable deterrent.

People
*   Death of Charles Newman, founder member of the Newport Athletic Club.

Places and Events

West Usk lighthouse was decommissioned and sold as a private dwelling. It was a popular place to visit for day trips when in use as its position gave a very good overview of Newport and the entrance to the River Usk from the Bristol Channel. The area on the top of the coastal bank was flat, grassy and easy walking and the air was 'bracing' (if you could stand the smell of seaweed!).

*   West Usk Lighthouse decommissioned.
*   Scouts first formed in Newport.
*   Trams began to run in Newport on a Sunday after seven refusals by the Council since 1903.
*   Trams and traffic used the temporary wooden bridge over the Usk (which was bought from London) until 1927, when the new bridge was completed.
*   Newport Council purchase Brynglas House to become a secondary school in 1925 and later became a Central School.
*   Beechwood Park Presbyterian Church rebuilt.

Beechwood Park Presbyterian church in Chepstow Road was rebuilt, at a cost of £7,000 and freehold £300. The original hall was built in 1906 and then became the Lecture Hall. This photograph was taken in 2007.

Health
- Woolaston House, Stow Hill was used as a hospital for the poor.
- Diphtheria, scarlet fever, whooping cough, measles, tuberculosis, typhoid and sleeping sickness swept through the town aided partially by the high temperatures and poor attention to personal hygiene.
- Visiting time in hospitals to see patients was very restricted with visiting on Adult wards only allowed between 3 and 4 pm on Wednesdays, Saturdays and Sundays and no visiting was allowed on children's wards and no child under 14 allowed to visit adults wards. All visitors had to obtain a ticket from the porter on the hospital gate. Each patient was allowed two tickets. This system was operated up until the 1950s. It was said this helped to cut down the transmission of infections. One nurse also reported remembering how they had to change their normal clothes when working on the wards … 'we had to change into their uniforms when on duty and change again on going home again. This was done to aid transmission of infections. Our uniforms were washed by the hospital'. Perhaps this would help with the MRSA problem of the 21st century!

1923

The British and Worldwide Scene, Events and People

- The Duke of York (later King George VI) married Elizabeth Bowes-Lyon in Westminster Abbey.
- Andrew Bonar-Law, British Prime Minister, died.
- Sir James Dewar, a chemist who invented the vacuum thermos flask, died.
- BBC broadcast its first weather forecast. The chimes of Big Ben were first broadcast.
- The first English Cup Final at Wembley stadium, London was played between Bolton and West Ham (2-0) before a crowd estimated to be 200,000. The stadium was knocked down in 2005/6. The first Cup Final in the New Wembley was in 2007 between Manchester United and Chelsea.
- Warren Harding, 29th American President from 1921-23, died. His presidency was tarnished by accusations of corruption in the government. He made a statement that has been used many times since, 'I could take care of my enemies but did not know how to cope with my friends'.
- An earthquake in Japan which left the city of Tokyo and Yokohama in ruins occurred on 1st September. Total of almost 100,000 people killed.
- Alexandre Gustave Eiffel, Paris, the French engineer who designed the Eiffel Tower, died aged 91. The Eiffel Tower was completed in 1889 for the celebration of the centennial of the French Revolution (1789-1799). The tower was made of 7,000 tons of iron in 18,000 parts held together by 2,500,000 rivets and rises to a height of almost 1,000 ft.
- Wilhelm Konrad von Röntegen, the German physicist who discovered X-rays in 1895, died. He won a Nobel Prize for his discovery in 1901.

The Local Scene, Events and People

Civic and Political

- The Mayor was Charles F. Williams.
- Ferdinand Arnodin, the French designer of the Transporter Bridge, visited the bridge.
- The first sod of soil was cut in readiness for starting the Talybont Water Scheme.
- Council decided to buy Belle Vue House, at the bottom of Belle Vue Lane which then became a residence for George Elliot MP. It was eventually demolished and the land incorporated into the Park.
- Council agrees to band concerts in Belle Vue and Beechwood Parks.

- Cenotaph, 40 ft tall, Clarence Place unveiled by Lord Tredegar on 2nd June.
- Wrought-iron gates were erected at the entrance of Rodney Parade together with a memorial plaque in memory of the 86 Newport Athletic Club members who lost their lives in World War I. It was re-dedicated in 2006 in a public ceremony.

The Cenotaph is a memorial to the 1,742 men and four women of the town who died in World War I and later also to those who died in World War II. The Cenotaph was built at a cost £2,296.

Gates and plaques at the entrance of Rodney Parade as a memorial to the 86 Newport Athletic Club members who lost their lives in World War I. The names of the fallen are shown on the plaques on the gates' pillars.

People

- W.H. Davies, the 'Tramp Poet', married Helen Paine. He presented some of his valuable works to the Newport Library.

Commerce

- HMS *Collingwood* and other large battleships were broken up at Cashmore's yard.

HRH The Duke of York, later King George VI served as a lieutenant on HMS Collingwood. At the Battle of Jutland she fired 84, 12 inch rounds and received no damage. In December 1922 she was sold for scrap. 40,000 people visited the ship before breaking started and the entrance fees of £817 were donated to Royal Gwent Hospital. It is said that the ship's masts were used by Mr A. Golledge, a builder, to support the roof and ceiling of the Roman
Museum in Caerleon. If they are still used for such they have been covered by plaster. Many houses had washing line poles and railings and other items sold by Cashmore's off some famous ships.

Places and Events
- Newport Playgoers Society formed.
- Motor omnibuses introduced on routes not served by trams.
- Newport Athletic grounds, Rodney Parade, was purchased from Lord Tredegar for £7,026; area of 15½ acres; covered stand erected.
- The *South Wales Argus* extend their High Street premises.
- Jack Wetter's Newport Rugby XV were invincible, 1922-23.

Health
- Proposal for a crematorium turned down as it was thought to be un-Christian to burn bodies.
- Springfield Mansion near the workhouse ceased was to be used as an isolation hospital and is converted to provide accommodation for nurses.

1924

The British and Worldwide Scene, Events and People

- Ramsay MacDonald became Britain's first Labour Prime Minister on 22nd June. He made the first election broadcast on the BBC.
- Wembley World Exhibition or British Empire Exhibition opened by the King in London on 23rd April. It was designed to show off British Industry. The British Empire contained 58 countries at that time, and only Gambia and Gibraltar did not take part. It cost £12 million. It was the largest exhibition ever staged anywhere in the world. It attracted 27 million visitors. It continued into 1925.
- BBC first used the 'pips' as a time signal from the Greenwich Observatory.
- Lenin (born 1870), the Soviet Communist leader, died. Russian city of Petrograd renamed Leningrad.
- The Eighth Olympic Games opened in Paris. Often referred to as the Liddell Games.

The Local Scene, Events and People

Civic and Political
- The Mayor was W. Ellis Robertson.
- Population was 96,726 (estimated) in 16,044 dwellings.
- The Duke of York visits the Transporter Bridge, 8th March.
- Eight Newport councillors rebuked for taking excessive expenses.
- Work starts on the new Newport Bridge. Estimated cost of £140,275, the actual cost was £250,000.
- Council buy 16½ acres of land to extend Coronation Park near the Transporter Bridge.
- Annual deficit of the Transporter Bridge was £7,046.
- The Rt Hon. James (Jimmy) Henry Thomas of George Street, Pill granted the freedom of the borough . As MP for Derby he became a member of Ramsay McDonald's Cabinet in 1923 and a very influential man. He always said that he was proud of a system that allowed an engine cleaner from a poor home to become an MP and possibly the Prime Minister. He almost reached his ambition to do this but for one indiscreet error of leaking a budget secret.

Commerce
- A river coal boat was swamped and sank near the Transporter Bridge and three men drowned as a result of the backwash from the *Glen Usk* pleasure steamer passing.
- YMCA in Temple Street praised for its work since it started five years before.
- Works or Street outing to the seaside in the charabanc was considered to be a great 'treat'.

People
- Trades Union Council urge the reinstatement of Mr A.B. Boon a teacher in Bolt Street School who had been a conscientious objector in wartime and was suspended from his post. Education Committee refused reinstatement.
- Pill boy fined for damaging a tree in Belle Vue Park.
- Death of councillor J.H. Dunn, Mayor in 1903. He was a respected business man and churchman.

Places and Events
- Duckpool Road Baptist Church constructed.
- The Tredegar Arms Hotel opposite the old *Argus* offices in High Street collapsed.
- Opening of Allt-yr-yn and Ridgeway avenues for housing, thought to be houses for the more well off families.
- 9,000 Sunday School children march through the town on Whit Monday morning. Churches were still well attended.
- Newport Labour Party bought a warehouse in James Street, Pill for meetings and offices.

Health
- Smallpox outbreak caused concern in Newport and area.
- Lord Tredegar opened the new 'Outpatients' Department of the Royal Gwent Hospital.
- Beechwood Hospital (opened in 1915) closed and is replaced by Cefn Mably Hospital for TB patients.

1925

The British and Worldwide Scene, Events and People

- Summer Time or Daylight Saving was introduced in Britain on 21st May, 1916 was made a permanent feature in 1925.
- Mrs Thatcher, the first woman Prime Minister from 1979-1990, was born in Grantham as Margaret Roberts, the daughter of a grocer.
- Construction was started on the building of the Mersey tunnel. It was eventually opened on 18th July, 1934.
- Madam Tussauds, the 'Wax Works Museum', London was burned down on 18th March. It was reopened in 1928.

The Local Scene, Events and People

Civic and Political
- The Mayor was C.T. Clissit.
- The first stone bridge over the River Usk built in 1800 was ready for demolition.

Commerce
- Spittles Cambrian Foundry, next to the Town Dock, destroyed by fire.
- Pill Baths proved a failure for lack of use.
- A house in Capel Street sold for £320 and a shop in Commercial Road for £1,300.
- Sangster's Circus visited the town. It was reported in the *Argus* that the circus was also in the town at the time of the Chartist riots in 1839.

People
- Mixed bathing introduced at Stow Hill Baths. Reports that both men and women enthusiastically took the plunge together for the first time!

Places and Events
- Spring Gardens Elementary School, Courtybella Terrace, Pill, became a Central School and renamed Belle Vue. There was accommodation for 520 scholars (mixed).
- 'Housey-Housey', forerunner of Bingo, first played in Newport at the Cattle Market in Pill.

- Mrs M.J. Hart JP becomes Newport's first Lady Councillor.
- 1,000 houses to be built at Graig Park, Malpas, by the Allied Building Co.
- The Hon. Gwyneth Morgan's body found in the Thames. She was the daughter of Lord and Lady Tredegar.
- Roman Catholic Church opened in Corporation Road area.
- Beechwood Park extension opened.
- Hatherleigh School, Lawrence Hill, opened, 200 mixed pupils. Fred Hando was the headmaster from 1925 to 1953. (He died in 1970.) It was known to be a school with a purpose and this was a lot to do with the vision of the headmaster. The children were called by their Christian names and boys and girls were taught in the same class, another thing which was innovatory for its time. The school was situated in an old mansion house. The building was closed in 1985 after being used as the lower school of St Julian's High School. Fred was a prolific writer and wrote a series of 795 articles for the *Argus* entitled 'Monmouthshire Sketchbook'.
- Part of the medieval cross that once stood at the junction of Stow Hill and Havelock Street, found in the river mud during the building of the new Newport Bridge. It was said to have been destroyed by Roundhead soldiers in 1643.

Health
- Wireless was installed in the wards of the hospital.
- The log book of the hospital recorded that 2,173 patients had been treated and 212 admitted to the Friars and 12,519 people attended as out-patients. The records say that the average daily cost per in-patient was nine shillings.

1926

The British and Worldwide Scene, Events and People

- Our present Queen Elizabeth II was born at 17 Brunton Street, London as Elizabeth Alexandra Mary. She was the eldest daughter of the future King George VI.
- The General Strike in Britain started in response to the national lock-out of coal miners. It ended after nine days, although miners stayed out until November.
- Scottish inventor, Logie Baird, gave the first public demonstration of television. Even with crude apparatus by 1924 he managed to transmit a flickering image across a few feet. On 26th January, 1926 he gave the world's first demonstration of true television before 50 scientists in an attic room in central London. Baird died on 14th June, 1946 in Bexhill-on-Sea in Sussex.
- First widows pension paid in Britain.
- Agatha Christie, the English novelist, disappeared from her Surrey home. She was later discovered staying in a hotel in Harrogate under an assumed name. She had no recollection of how she got there. She wrote the famous detective books of Poirot and Miss Marple.

- George Bernard Shaw refused to accept the Nobel Prize of £7,000 awarded to him a year earlier. He said, 'I can forgive Nobel for inventing dynamite, but only a fiend in human form could have invented the Nobel Prize'.
- A radio programme at 5 pm called 'Children's Hour' started on the BBC. It became very popular particularly when 'Uncle Mac' was the reader.

The Local Scene, Events and People

Civic and Political
- The Mayor was A.T.W. James. He had his own printing and stationery shop in Bridge Street and later York Place. He was elected to the Council in 1919. He had family connections with Llanthewy Road Baptist Church. He was a keen cricketer and played for Newport and was a leading batsman, member of the Athletic club and a well known rugby referee.
- Town Clerk was O. Treharne Morgan.
- Population was estimated as 98,748.
- Excavations proceed at Caerleon's Amphitheatre (*below*) by Mrs Tessa Wheeler, wife of Dr R.E.M. Wheeler (later Sir Mortimer Wheeler famous archaeologist), partly sponsored by the *Daily Mail* newspaper.

Commerce
- Trade was reported as 'good' at the docks with coal exports to France, Spain, South America and Egypt.
- Fifty small boats were licensed to gather the small coal washed down river from the washeries of the collieries up the Ebbw valley and collected at Fifoots point. Often 'illegal' collectors also gathered this valuable source of fuel in the days of the depression and resulting shortage of money.

Day out at the beach with 'the girls' in daring garb for paddling in the seaside. They all had 'sun hats' on perhaps they knew about the 'ozone layer' and the effects of ultra violet light and sunburn?

The 1920s/30s holiday clothes, blazer, cricket sweater, white or grey trousers (called 'flannels').

People

- W.H. Davies, the 'Tramp Poet', awarded an honorary doctorate by the University of Wales.
- Death of Father Hill, a highly respected and hard working Roman Catholic priest in charge of St Michael's Church, Pill. At his funeral the streets were thronged with mourners. He was instrumental in arranging for the building of the Father Hill Memorial School, Pill in 1929.
- Roy Burnett, one of the most popular outside halves ever to play for Newport RFC was born. He played 372 times for Newport, captaining them in 1952/3. He was also capped for Wales. He died in 1998 and his ashes were sprinkled on the pitch at Rodney Parade.

Places and Events

- Newport has 80 inns, 50 beer houses and 34 drinking clubs.
- The General Strike affects trade in the town.
- New modern church dedicated to Saint Julius and Aaron, who were Christians martyred by the Romans at Caerleon on 1st July, AD 303, was built at St Julian's Avenue. It was built to replace two temporary chapels built in 1891 at Caerleon and St Julian's.

- A new Ford 6-seater touring car cost £125.
- The *South Wales Argus* was reputed to be a 'Liberal Party' paper. It cost 1*d.* per day. The *Western Mail* was reputed to be a Conservative paper. It also cost 1*d.* per day.
- The *South Wales Echo* and also the *South Wales News Weekly* cost 1*d.*
- Residents were fined for not clearing snow from their premises.
- The Olympia cinema in Skinner Street, was one of the most popular places of entertainment in the town.
- The *South Wales Argus* reported that the Sunday School Whit Monday parade through the town began before 1833. Each year in the 1920s there were approx 10,000 children in the procession.
- Pavilion Concert Hall, top of Stow Hill, opposite the St Woolos Hospital opened.
- Cases of smallpox occur in Pill.

Sport for Ladies
- Ladies Keep Fit class using 'club swinging activities' and hockey.

Ladies hockey 1920s style. One lady even had a tie on.

Club swinging was like the aerobics of more recent times. Only one name is known, that of Edna Vaughan, second from left front row.

1927

The British and Worldwide Scene, Events and People

- Sheila Scott (1927-1988), was born. She was a British aviator and the first woman to fly solo around the world in 1966 in her Piper Comanche 260 plane called *Mythtoo*.
- A football league football match was broadcast for the first time, it was between Arsenal and Sheffield United.
- The first British veteran car rally took place in London with 43 cars starting.
- Fidel Castro, was born.
- Althea Gibson, the first black person to win Wimbledon (1957) was born.
- Leon Trotsky (1879-1940) the Russian revolutionary was expelled from the Communist party and exiled in 1929. He was murdered in 1940 by a Stalin assassin when he was in Mexico.
- Charles Lindbergh, the American aviator (1902-74), flies the Atlantic alone in 33 hours on 21st May. He later moved to Europe with his wife to escape the publicity surrounding the kidnap and murder of their two-year-old son in 1932.
- Canberra was made the new capital of Australia and inaugurated by the Duke of York on 9th May.
- John Godfrey Parry-Thomas died in a tragic land speed record attempt in 1927 on Pendine sands in his car called *Babs*. He was a friend and competitor of Malcolm Campbell to try to win the world land speed record.

The Local Scene, Events and People

Civic and Political
- The Mayor was Frank Quick.
- Alderman Thomas Parry made a Freeman of the Borough. He was a leading figure in the construction of the Talybont reservoir. He died in 1935.
- Council decided to buy land in Clytha Park for the erection of a Civic Centre.

- New Bridge over the River Usk opened (22nd June, 1927).

The new Newport bridge.

Commerce
- Cashmore Ltd buy more warships for breaking up. In 1925 they were breaking up submarines K2, K6 and H21. K2 was the second of this class and built in Portsmouth in 1915. On the 7th November, 1924, K2 collided with submarine H29 during exercises. K2 was sold on the 13th July, 1926 to Cashmore's after a distinctly unsuccessful career.

People
- 20-year-old woman rescued after making a suicide attempt by jumping from the Transporter Bridge. It was a notorious venue for suicides.
- Revd Edward Elliott of Alma St Bapt Church campaigned against 'the most brutal contests' of boxing. Ironically at the same time the Scouts from his church were taking part in the first Scouting Boxing Championship at Newport Athletic grounds.
- Royal Humane Awards to Frank Hopkins (Fredrick Street) and John Huish (Portland Street) for saving people from drowning. Hopkins also received the Albert Medal from the King. The Albert Medal award was discontinued in 1971.
- E.H. Temme, of Newport, swam the English Channel in 14 hours 29 mins. In 1927, the year the Channel Swimming Association was formed to oversee and authenticate attempts, E.H. Temme became the first man to swim in both directions. He later became the first to repeat that feat in 1934. He is the only man to have swum the Bristol and English Channel from both sides. The first woman to swim the Channel was American Gertrude Ederle in 1926.
- Kathleen Thomas was the first woman to swim the Bristol Channel from Penarth to Weston-super-Mare on 4th September, 1927. It took 7 hours 20 mins. She died in 1987. She taught swimming in a London School as a career. A plaque to commemorate this is on Penarth Pier and was erected in 2007.
- Birthday cards of the era were often coloured postcards.

These cards were sent to Edna Vaughan on her 21st birthday.

Places and Events
- 120 acres of land bought at the Coldra by the council, eventually to become the Ringland Housing Estate.
- Newport 'Round Table' formed for men between 18 and 45.
- Heavy snow at Christmas time.
- Cardiff City football team beat Arsenal 1-0 in the Cup Final. They were the first, and only, club to take the cup out of England.

Health
- The Royal Gwent Hospital announce that all patients (other than the poor) would be expected to contribute towards the cost of maintenance while in hospital.
- Cases of smallpox announced in some Newport areas.
- Schools were given talks on the precautions to be taken and so help to prevent tuberculosis. Before the days of penicillin and other effective drugs TB was a killer disease which was easily spread.
- TB was a feared in all communities. Those children recovering after barrier nursing in hospitals were often sent to 'Open Air Schools' where education was mixed with treatment and 'plenty of fresh air'. In one school in Tredegar Park the sight of children sleeping outside for an afternoon nap covered in blankets was common.
- Wealthy adults were often sent to Switzerland for mountain air recovery.
- *South Wales Argus* appealed for eggs as an Easter gift to Royal Gwent Hospital.

1928

The British and Worldwide Scene, Events and People

- The world's first colour TV transmitted by John Baird at the Baird Studio in London.
- Emmeline Pankhurst, the suffragette and founder of the Women's Social and Political Union of Suffragettes, died in London. The Suffragette movement was started by Emmeline and her daughter Christabel in 1903.
- Women were given the right to vote on the same conditions as men in Britain in 1928. The Representation of the People Act 1918 enfranchised women over the age of 30 provided they were local government electors, or the wives of local government electors. The Representation of the People Act (Equal Franchise) of 1928 enfranchised all women over 21 years old, on exactly the same conditions as those applied to men.
- The first 'automatic transmission' car passed road tests.
- Britain's first telephone box installed in London.
- German airship with 60 persons aboard crossed the Atlantic (15th October).
- The 9th Olympic games opened in Amsterdam and the 2nd Winter Olympic games opened in St Moritz, Switzerland.
- Chiang Kai-Shek became the President of Nationalist China. He and his supporters were forced out of mainland China to the island of Taiwan in 1949.
- Hirohito was crowned Emperor of Japan.
- The first Mickey Mouse cartoon, 'Steamboat Willie' was shown.

The Local Scene, Events and People

Civic and Political
- The Mayor was Walter Thomas Griffiths.
- Lord Tredegar gives 61 acres of his deer park at Cardiff Road to the council for the purpose of a park, to be known as Tredegar Park. Nominal rent of £2 per year.
- Motor omnibus continued to replace trams.
- Birthrate in Newport the lowest ever.
- Total enfranchisement of Newport women over the age of 21 in 1928 added 984 over-21s to the Borough voting list.
- Pensions of 10 shillings paid to people between 65 and 70 for the first time.

Commerce
- Lysaght's Institute at Corporation Road opened.

Lysaght's Institute on Corporation Road in 2007.

- William Royce Lysaght CBE, JP became Chairman in the Orb Steelworks complex and was responsible for the setting up the works when they moved from Wolverhampton in 1897, he also set up steel works in Scunthorpe (1912) and Australia (1921). One of the conditions of bringing the steelworks to Newport was the creating a communication with West Newport, by the use of the Transporter Bridge. For services to Newport he was awarded the Freedom of the Town in 1936 by the Mayor Bill Casey.
- During World War I he was Chairman of the War Trade Dept for which he received a CBE. In World War II the Orb Steelworks was on a high priority bombing list for German bombing raids.

People
- Councillor Peter Wright elected as first Labour Alderman.
- Much poverty in Pill and other areas of Newport.
- Poor children of the town continue to receive 'Hot Pot Meals' at Christmas.

Places and Events
- Home Nursing Association started at 88 Stow Hill.
- Council begin developing land at Maesglas for houses for 'the working classes'; 616 houses were built in eight years.
- Widening of Malpas Road commenced.

- Plans to build 300 houses at Bassaleg Road, Gaer, by the Allied Building Corporation. It was a vast open fields site. Where the Gaer shops are now was once a duck pond. The pub was then a large farmhouse belonging to the Thomas family.

Allied houses were made of grey concrete blocks or 'Breeze blocks'. Many later were rendered with plaster or painted, but they are still in widespread use throughout Newport in 2007. The one shown is the house of Kay Price in Gaer Park Road and is in the process of being modernised but some of the previous owner's kitchen ware was still in use when she purchased it. The Allied housing scheme helped alleviate the problems of housing outlined by Peter Wright more than a decade before.

- Stelvio House, Bassaleg Road bought by the Board of Guardians for a Children's Home.
- Hornby House, Pugsley Street opened as a Scout HQ.
- Commercial transport started to become motorized.

Bailey & Williams furniture removers' commercial vehicle. With thanks to John Bailey for the photograph of his father's business.

Health
- Councillors concerned with the overcrowding in Pill which was causing tuberculosis and other diseases and infections due to families living and sleeping in one room. Better housing was advocated, a long time after Peter Wright first asked the Council to do something about it. It was hoped that the building programme of the Allied Housing Estates could alleviate the problem in the long term but not immediately.

1929

The British and Worldwide Scene, Events and People

- The first area of 'Green Belt' was approved in Britain and was five miles of land near Hendon, Middlesex.
- The Grand National Steeplechase at Aintree, Liverpool had a record entry of 66 horses.
- The British largest airship the R101 flew its first trials.
- Leon Trosky (1879-1940) the Russian revolutionist was expelled from Russia. He settled in Mexico where he was assassinated in 1940 on Stalin's instructions by a man with a pick.
- The St Valentine's Day massacre took place in Chicago on 14th February when seven unarmed members of the Bugs Moran gang were murdered by Al Capone's gang disguised as policemen. Al Capone was a notorious gangster but was arrested eventually on a technicality over tax evasion and imprisoned until 1939. He died in 1947.
- The German airship Graf Zepplin completed its round the world trip.
- Wall Street financial crash in USA affected the whole world economy. It was known as 'Black Tuesday'.
- The Vatican City became an independent Papal State within the city of Rome.
- The volcano Vesuvius in Southern Italy erupted on 5th June. It also erupted in 1913, 1926 and 1944.
- The Monaco Grand Prix was first run at Monte Carlo and was won by William Grover-Williams.

The Local Scene, Events and People

Civic and Political
- The Mayor was W.H. Williams.
- The MP, James Walker, was elected the first labour MP to be returned for the Town. He defeated Reginald Clarry (Conservative).
- A children's library was opened in Temple Street, believed to be the first one in Newport for children aged 5-11. Some mornings there was a 'Story Time'.

Commerce
- Pill traders complain of 24 empty shops in Commercial Road.

Newport Public Libraries

PILLGWENLLY BRANCH LIBRARY

(TEMPLE STREET)

A JUVENILE LENDING LIBRARY

for Children between the ages of 9 and 15 years,
will be formally OPENED at this Branch by

His Worship The Mayor

(Councillor WALTER T. GRIFFITHS, J.P.)

ON

THURSDAY, MAY 16th.

Hours of Opening: Daily 5 p.m. to 8 p.m. except Thursdays
(not open) and Saturdays (open 10 a.m. to 12 noon and
5 p.m. to 8 p.m.)

The Library will be open for the Registration of Borrowers only
Daily 5 p.m. to 8 p.m. from Friday to Wednesday,
May 10th to 15th.

Library Tickets are available for any of the Libraries and
Readers who already possess Library Tickets, therefore
do not need to Register.

On day of opening books will be issued from 7 p.m. to 9 p.m.

The Pillgwenlly Reading Room will be Closed from
1 p.m. on Wednesday, May 15th, to 7 p.m. on
Thursday, May 16th.

By Order of the Committee,

JOHN WARNER, Chief Librarian.

R. H. JOHNS LTD., Printers, Newport.

One 'child user' of the library said in her old age 'this library was a lifeline to me to educate myself and try to get out of a culture that surrounded me with poverty and deprivation. I would often be the first person in the library after running over the stone bridge from Capel Crescent, sometimes I would borrow one book a day during school holidays and would sit on the stairs at home avidly reading them. I always liked to sit on the stairs when reading as it was one of the 'quiet' places in the house. The librarian knew me well. This process helped me to love reading and ended up as a teacher in a secondary school'. The motto at the apex of the building said 'Knowledge is Power' and it still is!

Father Hill School opened on 5th January 1930, four years after his death, and School closed in 1974 and demolished in 1987 but the remembrance of Father Hill remained as his influence was enormous in Pill and throughout Newport. He was born in London of Jewish parents but was converted to the Roman Catholic faith when he was 19. He studied in Calvario in Italy for 6 years before he was ordained in 1904. When he came to Newport he was at St Mary's, Stow Hill and became the first Parish Priest of St Michael's in Pill. He worked tirelessly in the community and when he died at the age of 52 in 1926, many said he had 'worked himself to death'. His funeral was one of the biggest seen in Newport.

People
- Malcolm Thomas, captain of Newport Rugby team, 1954-59, and a British Lion and Welsh International, was born. He made 280 appearances for Newport.
- William Henry Robinson made Chief Constable.
- Christmas 'hot pots' issued to Pill poor families.

Places and Events
- Father Hill memorial School, being built at Oswald Road, Pill, cost £15,000. Accommodation for 440 pupils. Father Hill was the first rector of St Michael's RC Church.
- The *Weekly Argus* reports that Pottery Terrace in Pill had once seen a flourishing pottery trade. The original pottery was off Skinner Street near Hope Chapel in the town centre.
- Houses in Maesglas in course of erection. Maesglas was called 'Little Moscow' because most of the building work was carried out in the bitter winter. It was probably the first time council houses were built with a bathroom in Newport.
- The Lyceum Theatre in Bridge Street and the Empire Theatre become cinemas.
- The Olympia cinema, Skinner Street, acquired by ABC Cinemas.
- The canal was a popular place to walk along and also a dangerous place for children to play.

Health
- 334 cases of tuberculosis causes alarm. One third of the patients died within three months of the infection.
- More cases of smallpox notified than for many years.

The Lyceum Theatre had a distinctive architectural style which has been lost in the replacement buildings in a later era. Note also the entrance to the underground toilets in front of the Queen's Hotel.

Chapter Five

The Nineteen-Thirties

The period leading up to World War II was interesting as there was a certain sense of improvement in living conditions, wealth and expectations during the 1930s. The effects of the depression of the 1920s had largely diminished. More housing was being built which could be afforded by the emerging 'middle class' and more affluent working class and more rentable accommodation was underway and expanding. Much of this was the building of council houses on large estates. Much of the progress was stifled by the onset of World War II in 1939 and building was largely discontinued until the war ended in 1945 as there was a shortage of materials and manpower.

There was a time of celebration of the Silver Jubilee of King George V in 1935, the sadness of his death in 1936 and the confusion of sovereignty over the episodes of Edward VIII and eventual coronation of the Duke of York to become King George VI in 1937.

In 1921 the school leaving age was 14 and the Hadow Report suggested it should rise to 15. At the end of the 1930s about 10 per cent of elementary school pupils were selected to go on to secondary education, the rest either remained in 'all age' schools or went to non-selective 'senior schools'. By the time of the Spens Education Act in 1938 the recommendations were for a three tier system of Grammar for the academically able, Technical schools for those with a technical and practical ability and a new sub-group called 'the Secondary Modern' schools. Some educationalists were apprehensive as they felt it could lead to a separation of social groups. Also for teachers they were afraid that they might be classified as people only able to teach a particular ability group.

1930

The British and Worldwide Scene, Events and People

- Princess Margaret was born on 21st August in Glamis Castle, Scotland. She married a 'commoner' Anthony Charles Robert Armstrong-Jones in 1960 but he was later made the Earl of Snowdon. He was also born in 1930.
- The *Times* newspaper included a crossword on a regular basis for the first time.
- William Rhodes became the oldest man to play in a test match for England at the age of 52 years 165 days.
- The luxury liner *Empress of Britain* was launched at Clydebank shipyards in Scotland by the Prince of Wales.
- The first cricket test match between England and New Zealand took place at Christchurch in New Zealand.
- The planet Pluto was discovered by an astronomer, Clyde William Tombaugh, in Arizona. Its existence was predicted by Percival Lowell in 1905. Because of its small size it was re-classified as a minor planet in 2006.

The 'Gipsy Moth' of Amy Johnson.

- Amy Johnson took off from Croydon on 5th May and flew the 11,000 miles to Darwin, Australia, landing on 24th May. The plane was a single engine De Haviland 'Gipsy Moth'.
- Mahatma Gandhi began a campaign of civil disobedience in India.
- The World Cup soccer competition was instituted. Thirteen countries entered and the cup was won by the host country, Uruguay.
- Frozen foods, developed by Clarence Birdseye were first put on sale in stores in Springfield, Massachusetts.

The Local Scene, Events and People

Civic and Political
- Mayor was Thomas Crowther.
- Population of Newport was 97,220.
- The general rate for the town was reduced by 1s. 6d.

Commerce
- Last working canal cargo boat passed through Rogerstone. The canals were losing their popularity to transport goods.
- Coal was brought down from the mining valleys to the many docks and wharfs but some of the dock closed in the 1930s and were filled in and a shopping area built over them. Some of the foundations of the buildings suffered from subsidence as the land was soft.
- Pill traders complained of the derelict look of Commercial Road. They also requested that the road between Maesglas and Pill be made up for use (this would take a few decades before it was made roadworthy).

People
- Roman Catholic population in Pill was 4,653 and 925 children attended St Michael's Roman Catholic School. The town's main Roman Catholic church was St Mary's Church, Stow Hill.
- Bryn Meredith, one of the most famous rugby hookers of all time was born. He played well over 100 games for Newport captaining them in 1958/59 and again in 1961/62. He gained 34 Welsh caps and captained Wales on four occasions. He was also a British Lion.

High Street station in the centre, on the right is the Savoy Hotel, demolished in 1938.

Places and Events
* New High Street railway station opened on land previously called 'Dragon Fields'.
* Fire Station at Maindee closed and building converted to a public library. Police Station remained.

Maindee police station and the library on the left.

- The style of the prams were for a 'coach built high pram' even for the children's dolls prams.
- Houses at Graig Park, Malpas were being built.
- Newport residents see the giant airship R100 fly over. One observer said 'it was magnificent but frightening as during wartime these could easily be used to bomb cities'.
- The Father Hill Memorial School opened in Oswald Road, Pill. Most of the £15,000 needed to build the school was raised by Father Hill, a priest in Pill from 1921-26.
- Scout Band called the Newport Baden Powell Band, formed. It was disbanded in 2003 after giving much service within the town.

Health
- New nurses quarters built at Royal Gwent Hospital costing £62,000. Demolished in 1997 but other accommodation was built.

1931

The British and Worldwide Scene, Events and People

- The British Sterling currency was taken off the 'Gold Standard'.
- Resignation of Labour Government and the formation of a coalition under Ramsay MacDonald.
- Census of populatin for England and Wales had 40 million, Scotland 4.8 million, Northern Ireland 1.24 million.
- An important Statute of Westminster clarified the full autonomy within the British Empire for Australia, Canada, Ireland, Newfoundland, New Zealand, and South Africa, all British dominions at that time.
- New Zoo opened in Whipsnade on 23rd May.
- A new Sadler's Wells theatre opened in London.
- First electric trolleybuses seen on London streets. They were quieter than trams as they ran on inflated tyres not iron wheels on tram lines. The overhead cables were very conspicuous.
- The Highway Code was first issued in Britain by the Ministry of Transport as the new road traffic act came into force on 1st April.
- Collapse of German banking system and 3,000 banks closed and unemployment reached 5.6 million.
- Thomas Edison, died at the age of 84. Thomas Edison was an American inventor of the phonograph (early form of record player) and the electric light bulb. He developed the world's first electric power station in New York in 1882.
- Empire State Building in New York completed on 1st May. It took 410 days to build and was constructed by mostly immigrant European workers (3,400 of them). It had 102 floors and was 1,472 feet tall (449 m).
- The legendary Russian ballerina Anna Pavlova (born 1881) died.

The Local Scene, Events and People

Civic and Political

- Mayor was Griffith J. Jones.
- Reginald Clarry (Conservative) defeats James Walker at the General Election.
- Worst storm ever seen in Newport, many parts of the town were flooded.
- Newport Police were provided with cars and motorcycles.
- Motorcycles were becoming common and used by the police force. Crash helmets were not in common use.

Newport police had a number of motorcycles as their fast response teams. They were also used 'on patrol' around the town or local areas, Bill Humphries is shown. It was said the best protection to cold and rain on long motorcycle rides was a thick layer of the Argus or brown papers under your overcoat! Also it was necessary to wear your cap back to front to prevent it being blown off.

Commerce

- The Arrow fuel works, near the Transporter Bridge, closed.
- About this time Star Brickworks in Caerleon was opened. Many of the houses in the Newport area used 'Star bricks'. The Caerleon area and St Julian's areas had clay pits as the clay was suitable for brickmaking.
- After 88 years of use the Old Town Dock was filled in.

People

- J.H. Thomas MP originally from George Street, Pill, was made Secretary of State for the Dominions and Secretary of State for the Colonies. He became a very influential politician.

Places and Events

- Double-decker buses seen on the street for the first time.
- The suggestion that one-man operated buses be used, was abandoned.
- Television comes to Newport. The *South Wales Argus* explains how it works.

Health

- Diphtheria causes concern with 227 cases in Newport.
- In February , Dr Garrod Thomas (born 1853) died.

Sport

- Baseball was popular in the 1930s and many teams and leagues were in existence.

1932

The British and Worldwide Scene, Events and People

- Great Hunger March of unemployed to London. Unemployment in UK reached 3 million.
- Malcolm Campbell (1885-1948) drove his car, *Bluebird*, to beat his own world land speed record by reaching 253.96 mph. He was a person who loved speed on land and water. He gained the world speed record on land and on water at various times during the 1920s and 1930s using vehicles called *Bluebird*. His son, Donald Campbell, was killed in 1967, attempting to repeat his father's achievements but his speedboat flipped and broke up when attempting a high speed run.
- Former Labour MP, Oswald Mosley, started his own political party, the British Union of Fascists.
- James Chadwick, a famous physicist, discovered the neutron (a neutral nuclear particle) when working in Cambridge University. He was awarded the Nobel Prize in 1935. His work led to a greater understanding of the composition of the nucleus of atoms.
- Amelia Earhart became the first woman to fly the Atlantic solo. She flew from Newfoundland to Ireland in just under 15 hours. The plane she was flying disappeared in 1937 while on an attempt to do a round the world trip.
- The first 'Mars Bar' was made in Slough and went on sale in the shops.
- President Roosevelt was elected as President of USA. In 1921 Roosevelt suddenly became ill with polio and on recovery he was left unable to walk without braces or a walking stick, but through his determination and the support of his wife, Roosevelt was seen as great success as governor of New York. He was chosen as the Democratic presidential candidate in 1932, easily beating his Republican rival, Herbert Hoover.
- Economic slump in America and 5,000 banks close and unemployment rose.
- Sydney Harbour Bridge (the world's widest) opened on 19th March.
- Eamon de Valera was elected President of the Republic of Ireland.
- The tenth Olympic Games opened in Los Angeles and the third Winter Olympic Games opened in New York.
- An international disarmament conference met in Geneva but achieved nothing.
- Iraq gained independence from Britain.

The Local Scene, Events and People

Civic and Political
- Mayor was Walter J. Wall.

Commerce
- Hundreds of unemployed men cleaned up the old engineering works, Mill Parade, in preparation for it becoming an unemployment centre.

- Large building programme of private houses in the lower Gaer. One builder was Tommy Hill. Housing was needed for the workers of the expanding Whitehead's Steelworks on Cardiff Road. One resident commenting on the situation later said, 'Our house had a large back garden and room to grow vegetables. [This became a necessity in the next decade when war was declared and fresh vegetables were in short supply.] We even grew vegetables in the front garden during war time. Our house had three bedrooms, it was a semi-detached house in Lyndhurst Avenue and cost £484 3s. 6d. The houses generally had no garages as the people had no cars. We had previously lived in rooms with my parents in Adeline Street, so we thought we were in heaven. We had to learn the skills of gardening as the garden was just a field but the potatoes in that first year were enormous. Everyone moved in about the same time from various places either in Newport or from up the valley and we all got on well together … it was a special time in our lives. We worried about the large mortgage we had taken out to buy the house. We had our mortgage with the "Monmouthshire" and each month paid the 19s. 6d. Our pay at the time was between £6-7 per week.'

Originally the only form of heating was a coal fire in each room although fires in the 'front room and bedrooms' were considered a luxury and rarely used. The main living room fire grate had a facility to cook on them, and they needed 'black-leading' regularly. The open fire made the best toast done on a toasting fork..... can you smell that aroma? I can as I write these words. From the bedroom windows you could look all across the Bristol Channel..

People

- Death of John Cashmore, founder of John Cashmore Ltd, shipbreakers of Pill. The firm was probably one of the biggest employers in Newport over the years and had broken up many ships.
- A plot to kill the politician and ex-Newport resident, Rt Hon. J.H. Thomas was found out. A young Irish Sinn Féin man was arrested.

Places and Events

- Tram and bus services on Christmas Day discontinued.
- Greyhound racing commences at Somerton Park. The land was purchased by Cardiff Arms Park.
- Newport County FC play their first game at Somerton Park against Leyton Orient.
- Order made to clear up Newport's 'Shanty Town' which had been created at Brooks Field, Liswerry to accommodate homeless families and destitute people.
- The 'Hot Pot' fund still helps Newport's poorest families.
- Y Demyl Welsh Baptist Church, Commercial Road, near Alma Street, closed. It was opened in 1844.
- St Thomas's Church, Maesglas, was erected as a 'tin' or corrugated iron building; cost £750; seating capacity 300.The site was given by Viscount Tredegar. This was rebuilt in the late part of the 20th century.
- Maindee Swimming Pool, planned at a cost of £20,000 (by the time it was built it cost double this amount).
- Possibly the only urban fox hunt ever seen in the history of the county up to that time was held in Pill as the foxes were stealing the people's chickens. Hundreds of people armed with sticks chased a fox through Pill into the river where it swam across to the other side.
- Penny tram fares increase to 1½d.
- Last of the Wool Fairs held at the Cattle Market in Pill.
- Redevelopment of the 'Old Green Crossing' prior to the building of Kingsway road.
- Cardiff Road along by the Royal Gwent Hospital had been through many developments over the years as road traffic increased.
- The Graf Zeppelin seen in the sky as it passes over the town, so large that it blotted out the sun.

On the morning of 3rd July, 1932, the mighty Graf Zeppelin passed over Newport. It passed over slowly and the throb of the engines could be heard. The son (Peter) of Mr Rees a Newport optician was on board as a passenger. It was 700 ft long and 100 ft wide. It had circumnavigated the world in 1929 in 20 days. It mapped many previously unmapped areas.

Left: Kingsway just before it opened.

Cardiff Road with the railway line in front of houses. Think of the Health & Safety implications!

1933

The British and Worldwide Scene, Events and People

- Arthur James Balfour, Conservative Prime Minister 1902-1905, died aged 89.
- Two British planes became the first to fly over Mount Everest.
- The idea of FM radio was invented but the first workable system for radio communication was put into action by the American inventor Edwin H. Armstrong in 1936.
- First pictures of the 'Loch Ness Monster' were taken. There are also many sketches of double-humped sea monsters varying in length from 20 to 40 ft.
- There was a financial crisis in America and the banks closed for four days and an embargo was put on the export of gold.
- The German Nazis announced that they would withdraw from the League of Nations.
- Adolf Hitler appointed German Chancellor on 23rd January and the Nazi party became the only legal political party in Germany.
- The Reichstag, the German Parliament building in Berlin, was destroyed by fire, believed to be deliberately started on 27th February by the Nazis.
- 25,000 people queued to see the Turin Shroud when it went on display to the public at Turin Cathedral for the first time in 400 years.
- Radio Luxemburg, a private commercial radio station containing adverts for products, broadcast its first programmes in English.

The Local Scene, Events and People

Civic and Political
- Mayor was Frank Humphries.
- For the first time in Newport's history all the magistrates who sat on the bench were female.

People
- It was reported that there were 10,000 unemployed in the town.

Places and Events
- The famous peacocks and other exotic birds in Belle Vue Park were removed and sold. Peacocks sold for £3 each.
- As an economy measure the music relayed via loudspeakers in Belle Vue Park was stopped so saving £400.
- Maesglas Institute, Cardiff Road built (it was put up for sale in 2007).
- Newport Pavilion cinema, top of Stow Hill, goes bankrupt and closes.
- St Julian's House, Caerleon Road, demolished. At one time it was the home of the well-known Firbank family.
- The Civil Service Sportsground opens at Bettws.
- The town's first Military Tattoo held at the athletic grounds, Rodney Parade.
- The Temperance Hall, Dock Street, turned into a cinema and called the 'Capitol'.

1934

The British and Worldwide Scene, Events and People

* Bread put on ration in Britain.
* The British liner *Queen Mary* was launched 26th September, 1934 in Clydebank, Scotland. The *Queen Mary* was built at the Scottish John Brown shipyard and after fitting out made its maiden voyage on 27th May, 1936. She carried over 2,000 passengers and had a crew of 1,100. Retired from service in 1967 and is now a luxury hotel in Long Beach, California. It made 1,001 Atlantic crossings. When in service she was one of the fastest ocean liners and held the record for crossing the Atlantic on a number of occasions with speeds of around 30 knots (34½ mph). During the war she carried troops from America.
* The first women's cricket test match took place in Brisbane between Australia and England.
* The first radio broadcast of a royal wedding took place. It was the wedding between the Duke of Kent and Princess Marina in Westminster Abbey.
* The first laundrette was opened in Texas by J.F. Cantrell and was called 'Washateria'.
* Bonnie and Clyde, notorious outlaws were killed in an ambush in Louisiana, USA. Over a two-year period from 1932-34, during the height of the Great Depression in America, Bonnie and Clyde evolved from petty thieves to nationally-known bank robbers and murderers. They were killed in an ambush in Louisiana, USA as they returned to their hideout.
* Hitler became dictator of Germany. Hitler's rival Ernst Röhn and hundreds of other influential Nazis were murdered by the SS special police in what was called the 'Night of the long knives'.
* In China, Mao Tse Tung's 'Long march' with his 100,000 strong communist army began as a result of harassment by the Nationalist army.
* Marie Curie, the double Nobel Prizewinner for her pioneering work of the widespread application of radioactivity, died of an illness that was diagnosed as pernicious anaemia, caused by over exposure to radiation.

The Local Scene, Events and People

Civic and Political
* The Mayor was William F.E. Smith.
* Death of Courtney, 3rd Baron Viscount Tredegar, aged 67. Son of Evan, 2nd Baron Viscount, he continued his father's habit of extravagance.
* Borough extended to take in 2,853 acres of St Woolos parish.

People
* Death of councillor Peter Wright, world famous wrestler, sportsman, mayor, linguist, traveller, soldier, lecturer, philosopher, orator, etc. First Labour alderman, second Labour mayor. A teetotaller, who dined with

kings and emperors and had spent time in prison! He once refused a MBE from the King. A man 'of the people and for the people'.

* Death of Alderman Blackburn, whose building firm had erected many buildings in the town including St Stephen's Church, Alexandra Road, St Michael's Church, Clarence Street, the King's Head Hotel, Pant-y-Reos reservoir, Newport Arcade and many other buildings.
* The Mayor's Boot Fund distributed 1,051 pairs of boots to the very poor of Newport.

Places and Events

* High Street widened as volume of traffic increased.

The High Street. towards the bridge. Notice the contrast of a Rolls-Royce car on left and horse-drawn cart on right. The slow movement of horses led to traffic congestion.

* Popular Bullmoor Lido opens at Caerleon and a similar open-air swimming pool opened at Allt-yr-yn.
* More houses being built at Maesglas.
* St David's Roman Catholic Church, Cardiff Road, built.
* The Jewish Synagogue in Francis Street, Pill to close and transferred to Queen's Hill. The Jewish population of Newport declined by 50 per cent.
* New Tredegar Wharf School, Pill opened. Built on the site of the old school which was constructed in 1873.
* New bowling green opened at Belle Vue Park.
* Exciting and innovatory outing given by the boss of Wardley's Ladies Hairdressers (corner of Bridge Street and Careau Road) to its staff , that of a flight from Cardiff to Bournemouth in the 'state of the art' passenger plane!

This was considered to be a very adventurous outing and received publicity in the local paper. Perhaps that is what the owner wanted! Crowd contained Marjorie Parry, Harold Wardley, Trevor Jones, Marjorie Roberts, Billy Nash.

Health
- Tuberculosis was on the decline within the population of Newport but cancer increased.
- There were 'open air schools' for children thought to be vulnerable to TB and other breathing related complaints and these were often in the town's parks. The children had camp beds outside in the air and every afternoon they were made to have a sleep in the open air covered by blankets. Many children envied such children to be able to play in the park all day and have a sleep. One such park was in Tredegar Park. The exact date of their start and end is not known but a reader of this book might have been one of the pupils or known someone who was.

1935

The British and Worldwide Scene, Events and People

- The Silver Jubilee of King George V was celebrated on 6th May.
- Baldwin succeeded MacDonald as Prime Minister of UK on 7th June.
- Lawrence of Arabia died as a result of a motorcycle accident. He was born in Tremadog, North Wales in 1888.
- The 30 mph speed limit introduced on British roads. Mr Leslie Roles of Mill House, Llangelly was the first person in Gwent to be fined £1 for speeding.
- 'Radar' (Radio Detection and Ranging) was first demonstrated in Daventry. This was to become an essential tool in enemy plane detection in World War II.
- The RAF's first monoplane fighter, the Hawker 'Hurricane', made its maiden flight.
- Land speed record of 301 mph made by Malcolm Campbell.
- Nylon was first manufactured by DuPont by a research team containing Gerard J. Berchet and Wallace Carothers
- London adopts a 'Green Belt' policy for the capital and kept many of the open areas and large parks.
- Hitler violated the Versailles Treaty of 1919 and orders conscription into the military forces in Germany.
- Pioneering aviator Amelia Earhart became the first person to fly solo from Hawaii to the United States.
- The game of Monopoly went on sale and became the world's most successful board game.

A Monopoly game of 1940s with the original money, cards and 'the boot'. One 'Chance' card says 'Speeding Fine, £15' and a 'Community Chest' card says 'Doctor's Fee £50' (that was more than a months pay for a typical worker). Rent in Park Lane was £175 with one house on it and Whitechapel £20 and The Angel, Islington £6 ... bargain prices!!

The Local Scene, Events and People

Civic and Political

* Mayor was William Casey, he opened the Hospital Fete.

Each year a Carnival Queen was chosen along with a set of 'courtiers' and it was a great prize to win such a competition and to 'reign' during the period of the carnival and fete. It was every child's dream to be a courtier and young ladies' ambition to be the 'Queen'. Some of the carnival entrants are in the photo along with the Mayor.

* Reginald Clarry (Conservative) defeats John Bowen (Labour) at the General Election by 2,000 votes. He was knighted in 1936.
* South Tower of Newport Castle was under the care of Office of Works and the remains of the brewery were cleared away.
* Number of vehicles registered 9,647 (double that of 1921: one vehicle per 25 residents).
* Driving tests were introduced in Britain by Leslie Hore Belisha and 'L' plates were made compulsory for learner drivers in Newport. Prior to that all a person had to do was to buy a driving licence at the post office.
* Birching still a form of punishment for the young but opposition grows.
* Borough boundary extended to Allt-yr-yn, Gaer, Ladyhill Liswerry, Malpas and St Julian's.
* Decision taken to build the Civic Centre at Clytha Park.
* Silver Jubilee of King George V and Queen Mary extravagantly celebrated. Mass demonstration of school children at the athletic grounds, Rodney Parade; street parties, etc.
* Shaftesbury Hotel building was removed allowing an uninterrupted view of the castle.

Commerce

* Unemployment 10,227.
* Ocean liner, SS *Doric*, purchased by John Cashmore Ltd for breaking up. Bought by Cashmores for £50,000, the ship was opened for the public to view and the proceeds from the entrance fees given to the Royal Gwent Hospital. A number of ships were opened to the public before breaking up and John Cashmore was a good donor to the Hospital funds

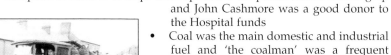

* Coal was the main domestic and industrial fuel and 'the coalman' was a frequent visitor to the streets.

James Parry was one of the coal merchants of the town and the 112 lb. (or one hundredweight) bags needed a lot of strength to carry to the door and empty in the 'coalhouse'.

People
- Death of Alderman Thomas Parry, previously registrar of births, deaths and marriages in the Borough. A well respected citizen.
- Alderman Sir John Moxon made a Freeman of the Borough.

Places and Events
- Newport Playgoers Society buy St James Church, Dock Street and convert it to 'The Little Theatre'.
- Mission to Seamen in Temple Street, Pill (*right*), celebrated its centenary.
- Foundation stone of the new Holy Cross Roman Catholic School, Emlyn Street was laid. Cost of school £17,000. The first school on the site was built in 1874.
- Portland Street Methodist chapel, Pill closes.
- Church Hall opened at Maesglas as a Sunday School for St Thomas's Church.
- Bassaleg High School opened.

Health
- Measles epidemic struck the town mainly among the children.
- Royal Gwent Hospital made an appeal for £80,000. Up until 1948 the hospital was run entirely by voluntary contributions.

1936

The British and Worldwide Scene, Events and People

- King George V died at Sandringham aged 70.
- Mrs Wallis Simpson obtained a divorce from her second husband.
- In the USA the first pop music chart was compiled.
- The first televised gardening programme was broadcast by the BBC, called 'In Your Garden' and presented by Mr Middleton.
- Leslie Mitchell became the first TV announcer in Britain when he announced the BBC programme at the Berlin Olympics.
- Elizabeth Cowell was Britain's first woman TV announcer at Alexandra Palace studios.
- The famous 'Jarrow March' of unemployed shipyard workers started in Jarrow (Tyneside) and marched to London. The Jarrow marchers presented a letter of protest about unemployment to the Prime Minister. They were led and supported by Ellen Wilkinson MP.
- The Crystal Palace glass building at Sydenham, South London, was destroyed by fire on 3rd November. The original Crystal Palace was built in Hyde Park, London for the 1851 Great World Exhibition.
- The first 'Open Prison' in Britain was opened in New Hall near Wakefield.
- The 'speaking clock' was introduced by GPO. It was known by its dialling letters as 'Tim'.

- The first British high definition television was broadcast from the BBC studios at Alexandra Palace.

TVs were first available about 1936 but only the wealthy could afford them. The screen was 9 or 12 inches and was the end screen of a cathode ray tube. Compare with the size of the hand. They really became popular and more available in the post-war years and were in great demand in the 1950s and particularly for the Coronation of Queen Elizabeth II. People would gather around a small TV and be amazed at the black and white pictures. Sometime a large water-filled magnifying glass was put in front of the screen to increase the size of vision.

- The Spanish Civil war between the Fascists and Republicans started on 8th July and General Franco later took office as head of the Nationalist Government. The war ended on 1st April, 1939. Franco died in 1975. Many volunteers from Newport and the coalfields joined the Republican side in the Spanish Civil War so opposing the extreme right wing Spanish Generals. Many died for the cause.
- The 11th Olympic games opened in Berlin and the Winter games in Garmisch-Partenkirchen, Germany. Jesse Owens won four gold medals for sprinting, he was said to be the fastest runner in the world.
- The 'Spitfire' plane was first flown by Capt. J Summers. It was a vital plane in the Battle of Britain in World War II as it was light and made largely of lightweight metals, like aluminium and balsa wood frame and due to its power to weight ratio was able to out-manoeuvre the German fighter planes.

The Local Scene, Events and People

Civic and Political

- The Mayor was Isaiah Vincent.
- Population 99,921.
- Reginald Clarry MP, knighted.
- Thirty-three emergency police call boxes erected throughout the borough.
- J.H. (Jimmy) Thomas, who became Labour MP for Derby and a member of the Cabinet and who was born in George Street, Pill was accused of divulging confidential budget secrets and resigned his seat as an MP and retired from political life, returning to live in South Wales.
- A 'Rat Week' organized in the town and thousands of rats were killed.
- Council decide to scrap all trams in favour of buses. The last tram actually ran in September 1937.
- Councillor Fred Phillips, William Royce Lysaght and Alderman John Davis made Freemen of the Borough.

Commerce

- T. Cecil Howitt & Partners, architects, win competition for the design of the Civic Centre.
- St Barnabas Church, New Ruperra Street, Pill, reopens.

People

- A celebrated landmark, the Eveswell fountain and water trough at the bottom of Batchelor Road, Maindee, was accidentally demolished by a truck. The legend goes that the well connected with this landmark was named Eves-well as it became linked with the small village of Whitsun (just outside Newport) where lived a girl named Eve. She died and reappeared as a ghost which, when being exorcised, made off across the moors towards Newport. Arriving at the place of the well in Maindee she escaped her pursuers by diving into the waters of the well and was seen no more. Since then the area was described as 'Ffynon Eva' or Eveswell and Eveswell Street and School are named after it.

Places and Events

- Greyhound racing popular at Somerton Park.
- Holy Cross Roman Catholic School opened in Emlyn Street.
- St Paul's Church, Commercial Street, celebrated its centenary.
- The Roman Catholic junior school at St Michaels Street, Pill opens. Cost £5,500.
- Kingsway by-pass between Town Bridge and Cardiff Road opened.
- Forge Lane between Newport and Bassaleg becomes the first dual carriageway in Gwent. During the works the 'Bassaleg Turnpike' road was demolished.
- 16th January - fierce storms and the highest tides for 40 years, some areas of Goldcliffe and Maindee and areas of the town were flooded. One of the authors was born on the 17th and his mother claimed it was because of 'the fright of the electric storms' the day before.
- Newport Cricket Club celebrated its centenary.

Health
- Some families had health schemes paying a few pence a week into a health fund to help pay the bills should sickness or hospital care be needed. The Royal Gwent Hospital Fund had (and still has) a building opposite the main gate of the hospital.
- Some doctors in the poorer areas would charge very little and often gave their services free to many. There were some very caring doctors who saw their role as a family support and care worker as much as a medical doctor, such as Dr Lilian Griffiths in Pill and others. She knew all her patients personally and the patients had confidence in what she said had to be done.

1937

The British and Worldwide Scene, Events and People

- Coronation of King George VI and Queen Elizabeth in Westminster Abbey on 12th May.
- The Duke of Windsor, who abdicated as King Edward VIII, married Mrs Wallace Simpson in France in June.
- The Duke and Duchess of Windsor arrived in Berlin and met Hitler. This led to much speculation and concern in Britain.
- A coalition government was formed under the leadership of Neville Chamberlain.
- Salaries of MPs raised from £400 to £600 pa on 22nd June.
- Ramsay Macdonald, the first British Labour Prime Minister in 1924, died at sea when on a 'health cruise'.
- Billy Butlin opened his first holiday camp. Remember the 'Red Coats' and the wake-up call? The chalets were often better and more luxurious than the homes of the time.
- Frank Whittle tested his invention of a jet engine on a test bed on the ground.
- The British aircraft carrier *Ark Royal* was launched at Birkenhead. She was an active participator in many wartime battles but was eventually sunk by a German U81 torpedo in 1941. All but one member of the crew were saved; 1,487 survived.
- First frozen foods went on sale in Britain.
- First London Motor Show opened. Cars were beginning to be seen as a possible means of transport for the family. Prices for a small car was approximately the annual wages of a worker.
- Lawn Tennis at Wimbledon was televised for the first time.
- '999' emergency telephone number came into operation in Britain.
- The first British quiz programme, an inter-regional spelling competition, was broadcast on the radio.
- A 500,000 ton asteroid shot past the Earth missing it by 485,000 miles. This was considered to be a 'near miss' in astronomical terms.
- Walt Disney's 'Snow White & the Seven Dwarfs' was shown in Los Angeles and became the first full length talking cartoon picture.

- Spanish Civil War continued and was supported by an 'International Brigade' made of many artists, writers and academics wanting to strike back at the Fascists. Ernest Hemingway was one writer and sent news back to America. He eventually committed suicide just like his father.

The Local Scene, Events and People

Civic and Political

- In May the town was well decorated to celebrate the Coronation of King George VI and Queen Elizabeth.
- The next Mayor chosen was Alderman Mary Ann Hart (1874-1967), (she was the first Lady Mayor and first lady Alderman).

Mary Hart as well as being a Mayor and an Alderman also had the unique honour of being admitted to the Gorsedd at the Welsh National Eisteddfod in Cardiff in 1938 and also awarded an OBE. She took on the title of Mair Gwenlli or Mayor of Pillgwenlly. She lived in Lewis Street. It was said her front room was always open for advice to the people requiring it and many people benefited from her advice and wisdom.

- The 'Little Theatre' in Dock Street opens on 11th January, a few yards from the Public Library. Entrance fee half a crown (2s. 6d.). The first play to be performed there was 'And So To Bed' about the life of Samuel Pepys, considered to be a risqué play at the time.

- King George VI and Queen Elizabeth came to Newport on 14th July.

King and Queen arrived at Newport station to visit the site and to cut the first sod of earth for the building of the Civic Centre. This was the first visit by a reigning monarch to Newport for a few hundred years.

Commerce

- Newport Electricity has nearly 25,000 customers and opens a showroom in High Street.
- The Allied Houses to rent were being built at Graig Park, Malpas.
- Last tram (No. 51) left Corporation Road for Alexandra Dock at 10.15 pm, 5th September, 1937. It had been the method of communal transport in Newport for 34 years.
- Construction work begins on the new Civic Centre only to be interrupted by World War II in 1939.

The last tram at the Westgate loaded with passengers who wanted to be on the last tram trip in Newport.

The last of the old trams, No. 51, being towed away on a trailer to be taken to Cashmore's yard in Pill for breaking up. The tow truck belongs to Wynns of Newport, a heavy haulier firm.

People

- Hundreds of residents enjoy sea trips across the Bristol Channel from the landing stage at Rodney Parade on the P. & A. Campbell boat.
- Some Basque children evacuated from Spanish Civil War (1936-1939) take up residence in Cambria House, Mill Street, Caerleon.
- Street Parties to celebrate the Coronation of King George VI and visits by the mayor. Newport hung up decorations.
- Refereee T.H. Vile was made President of the Welsh Rugby Union. Tommy II. Vile was born in 55, Alma Street in 1882. After he left school he joined his brother in the family firm of Vile Bros, manufacturers of 'Pop' in their factory between Lewis and Alma streets. He played rugby for Pill Harriers then to Newport and earned international status between 1908 and 1921 and made 198 appearances for Newport. On retiring from playing he took up refereeing. In 1937 he was elected the President of the Welsh Ruby Union, he was also President of Newport Rugby Club. In World War I he served as a captain in the Royal Artillery. In 1944 he was made a JP and also awarded an MBE. He died in 1958.

Coronation Party Adeline Street 1937. Some people are Mr and Mrs Manship, Oliver Jones, Lily Williams, Mrs Haley, Jimmy Evans, Mrs Elizabeth and Mary Harold and Mrs Gough.

Places and Events
- Horses still used as a means of transport for commercial purposes. Hicks the undertakers still used horse-drawn carriages as it 'looked more dignified' for a funeral.
- A record attendance of 24,268 fans witness Newport County FC draw 1-1 with Cardiff City FC at Somerton Park on 16th October in the Football League Third Division South.
- Newport Athletic Club had a very successful Hockey team. John Berthon was probably the most influential member of the team and club. Bill Griffiths was selected for the British Olympic team in 1938.

1938

The British and Worldwide Scene, Events and People

- Neville Chamberlain (British Prime Minister 1937-40) returned from the Munich Pact meeting waving a letter signed by Hitler which Chamberlain said guaranteed 'Peace in our time'. This was not going to be the case. He was succeeded as Prime Minister in 1940 by Winston Churchill.
- The Munich agreement under which Czechoslovakia was compelled to hand over part of its territory to Nazi Germany was signed by Britain, France, Italy. This was supposed to prevent further war. The agreement was not kept by Germany which annexed Czechoslovakia in 1939. Dr Eduart Benes, the president of Czechoslovakia resigned and fled abroad.
- Gas masks were issued to Britain's civilian population in anticipation of a war with Germany.
- The British Navy was mobilised and many ex-Navy and Merchant Navy people were called up for service. Those too old were placed in related jobs like plotting naval convoys for the Ministry of Defence. There was an office doing this in Stow Park in Newport.
- The British liner the *Queen Elizabeth* was the largest passenger liner ever built up to that time and was launched at Clydebank in Scotland on 27th September.
- The liner the *Queen Mary* gained the 'Blue Riband' by sailing the Atlantic in a record West to East time of 3 days 20 hours on 14th August.
- The English Cup Final at Wembley between Preston North End and Huddersfield was the first to be televised.
- The WVS (Women's Voluntary Service) was started in Britain by the Marchioness of Reading. It became 'Royal', RWVS, in 1966.
- The first edition of the *Beano* comic went on sale in Britain.
- The British Naval base in Singapore was opened.
- The Auxiliary Territorial Service (ATS), the female branch of the army, was formed by Royal Warrant.
- Toothbrush bristles were manufactured in Jersey and became the first commercially manufactured product made of nylon.
- The first breath tests for suspected drunken drivers were introduced officially by the Indianapolis Police Dept, USA.

- 'Kristallnacht' in Germany when the Nazis burned 267 synagogues and destroyed thousands of homes and businesses of Jews.
- The beautifully streamlined railway engine *Mallard* sped to 126 mph, a world record for a steam engine.

The Local Scene, Events and People

Civic and Political
- Incoming Mayor was John Robert Wardell.
- Air raid precautions given priority in view of the fear of war. Air raid wardens were being recruited in all neighbourhoods. They were issued with helmets and navy uniform and a whistle. They were called the ARP corps.
- 13,623 school children in the Borough; 90.8 per cent attend schools regularly.
- 96,000 gas masks stored at the old Tivoli cinema, Commercial Road, Potter Street.

People
- Unveiling ceremony with Mr and Mrs W.H. Davies at Church House, Portland Street, of a plaque commemorating his visit at the place he once lived. His book *The Autoboiography of a Super-Tramp* was published in 1908. One of his poems contains the verse, … 'Can I forget the banks of Malpas brook, Or Ebbw's voice is such a wild delight, As on he dashed with pebbles in his throat, Gurgling towards the sea with all his might'.

Mr and Mrs W.H. Davies accompanied by John Masefield (Poet Laureate) attending the unveiling ceremony at Church House, Portland Street, Pill. He donated many scripts and books to Newport Library.

Places and Events
- The first public air raid shelter was completed in Brunel Street adjoining the Transporter Bridge anchorage.
- Mission to Seamen's Hostel opened at Alexandra Dock.
- Maindee swimming pool opened.
- Concerts allowed in Town cinemas on Sundays.
- The Odeon cinema, Clarence Place, built and opened.
- Ebbw Bridge Baptist Church, Cardiff Road, established.
- At Jays Furnishers (near Newport Bridge) a three piece suite costs less than £10 or one shilling a week.
- A return train fare to Scotland for the Rugby International cost £1 2s.
- A four-bedroom house in St Woolos Road costs less than £550 and a new Standard nine car £150.
- The Empire Theatre in Charles Street was charged with allowing a lewd and indecent act when a young lady appeared on stage covered only in a layer of grease paint.
- The old Savoy building, Station Approach, was demolished to make way for the Post Office extension in High Street. This is yet another of Newport's well known buildings destroyed for an inferior looking building.

1939

The British and Worldwide Scene, Events and People

- Much of the British and world news was to do with the preparation for the war.
- Coldest winter months in Britain since 1894.
- Earthquake in Chile, 30,000 people killed on 25th January.
- King George VI launches the battleship *King George V* on 21st February.
- Bohemia and Moravia annexed by Hitler (16th March).
- Conscription was introduced in Britain on 28th April and compulsory military service for all men aged 20 to 41 on 2nd September.
- Transatlantic airmail service was started (May 20th).
- Italy leaves the League of Nations. Italy and Germany sign a pact on 2nd May.
- Anglo-Polish treaty was signed on 25th May.
- British fleet mobilised in August.
- Nazi-Soviet pact was signed in Moscow approving the partition of Poland (24th August).
- Holland mobilised on 28th August.
- Hitler declares war on Poland and attacks it (1st September). This provokes other countries to declare war on Germany including Britain and France.
- Evacuation schemes put into motion in Britain and 1,200,000 families moved from areas thought to be vulnerable to heavy bombing to more rural areas. Key workers remained in the locations (1st-3rd September).
- On 3rd September, 1939 Prime Minister Neville Chamberlain announced that Britain was now at war with Germany.

- The British liner *Athena* sunk by a German submarine off the coast of Ireland (4th September).
- Identity cards introduced in Britain (National Registration Act - 5th September).
- Britain experienced its first air raids of the war on 6th September.

To help the police identify anyone in Britain people were asked to carry their identity cards wherever they went. They were about twice the size of a credit card and many got quite damaged due to them being put in wallets and pockets. They had to be presented whenever challenged to do so by a policeman. They contained little helpful information other than name and address, an identity number and a signature.

- British troops enter France on 11th September.
- Petrol rationing started on 22nd September and only 'essential users' were entitled to petrol coupons.
- Sigmund Freud, Austrian psychiatrist dies in London aged 83 (23rd September).
- The Royal Navy battleship *Royal Oak* was torpedoed and sunk in Scapa Flow with the loss of 810 lives (14th October).
- Russia invaded Finland on 30th November.
- The famous battle of the River Plate took place on 13th December and the naval ships involved included the cruisers *Exeter*, *Ajax* and *Achilles* which took on the German battleship *Graf Spree*. The latter was eventually scuttled in the entrance to Montevideo harbour.
- Russia was expelled from the League of Nations (14th December).

The Local Scene, Events and People

Civic and Political
- Mayor was Richard Davies.
- Population 96,620.
- A well-known Newport landmark, the World War I tank, at Livingstone Place, Chepstow Road, was cut up for scrap to aid the war effort of producing armaments for the defence of the country.
- Home Guard were formed and the Newport Athletic Club became a Civil Defence Depot.
- Blackout restrictions were imposed and shop and street lights were either removed, covered or dimmed with shades pointing to the floor. Car headlights also had masks directing light downwards. It was a dark and depressing time in Newport. The sale of hand torches did well.
- Because of the ordnance factories and steel and coal industries and the docks it was feared that Newport would be a prime target for German bombings so barrage balloons sites appeared at strategic points throughout the town to help prevent low flying planes.
- The Military (Compulsory) Training Act of Parliament enforced and many young Newport men registered for military service at the Rodney Parade Employment Exchange.

- Newport prepared for hostilities. Air raid sirens were tested, blackout introduced, ration books issued, almost six miles of trenches were dug in open spaces, car parks, public parks, to cater for 10,000 people and air raid precautions given top priority. Thousands of gas masks were distributed and public air raid shelters were built. Shops and houses with deep basements were signposted as possible air raid shelters.

Ladies Gas mask and 'handbag' carrying case supplied by Val and Roy Evans.

- The Assize Court transferred from Monmouthshire to Newport on 6th November.

Commerce
- Godins works established next to Whitehead's Iron and Steel Co. works at Mendalgief Road and take over the Pill Harriers sports ground, which the latter had occupied since 1893.
- Newport Schools still operate a sex separation policy in schools and classrooms.
- Work commenced on the Royal Ordnance Factory at Clark's Fields, off Corporation Road, later in 1946 to become Standard Telephone & Cables Ltd.
- The famous liner *Balmoral Castle* arrives at Cashmore Yard Pill for breaking up. Many homes had pieces of furniture, deckchairs, line poles made from metal rails etc. bought from Cashmore's. Some items still had the names engraved on them.

People
- Evacuated Basque children living in Cambria House, Caerleon help in the war effort by filling sandbags. Also volunteers from schools do the same thing.
- Everyone urged to carry their gas masks and tin hats if they possessed one. Also a first aid kit should be carried and a larger one in the home was recommended.
- Many women knitted scarves, gloves and balaclava hoods for soldiers. Old knitted jumpers were undone and the wool used for these and other items.

Places and Events
- Newport County AFC promoted to the Second Division of the Football League but only played two games because of the outbreak of the war.
- Official opening of Talybont reservoir (1st July), 16 years after it was started.
- Pill Harriers RFC played their last game on the old ground and the club temporarily disbanded due to war duties.
- Foundation stone of St Julian's High School was laid at Heather Road. Pupils from the Municipal Secondary School (previously called Higher Elementary School and Newport Secondary School) moved into the completed building in 1941.

- Female policewomen employed for the first time.
- Shops in town with underground basements were asked to make them available as air raid shelters for shoppers and signs were erected with directions.
- The disused Portland Street Methodist Chapel (closed 1936) becomes an Air Raid Precautions (ARP) store.
- Plaque unveiled in Thomas Street opposite the King's Head Hotel, High Street to commemorate the birth of John Frost who was born in the Royal Oak public house.
- Maindee cinema, Chepstow Road, opened and could seat 1,189 people. Later it became a Bingo Hall and then a public house.
- Anderson air raid shelters erected in gardens of houses.

Shelters were named after Sir Thomas Anderson, the Home Secretary. The shelters would not withstand a direct hit but they did have the advantage that no ceilings, broken glass, roofs and bricks could fall on you. The person in 'plus fours' was the Deputy Borough Engineer Colonel Arthur Borlace with Bill Powell the works foreman on the left.

An Anderson shelter in a garden in the Gaer. It was covered in earth and eventually grass and flowers grew on top of it. The two girls were Glenys Critchley and June Thomas, the lad was one of the authors! The shelter went underground by about one metre and the earth dug out was put on top and eventually a 'raided' flower garden covered the metal sides. It always smelt damp inside.

Health

- The Royal Gwent Hospital had an overdraft of £91,000. Running costs were £100 per day. The hospital had accommodation for 400 patients. Hospital commemorates the opening of 'The Dispensary' 100 years earlier in Llanarth Street.
- Hospital prepares for casualties and a strategy in case of heavy bombings. Sand bags were used to cover certain areas and the windows were all blacked out and criss-crossed with sticky tape to avoid splinters of glass if they were smashed with bomb blast. Any basement rooms were also cleaned and prepared for evacuation in case of a bomb raid.

Chapter Six

The Nineteen-Forties

The period covering World War II is extensively covered in many other books and this publication will not reiterate them in any great detail but some events will be mentioned as they impinge on local life.

Some personal accounts of how the war affected the people of Newport are included.

To help finance the war various forms of 'National Savings' were encouraged and special campaigns each year helped to focus on these, e.g. 'Spitfire Week'. Any household with a garden or allotment holder was encouraged to 'Dig for Victory' and help to supply fresh food because imported food from overseas was affected by the enemy sinking the supply ships. Many lawns and flower gardens were converted to vegetable patches and schools often had mini gardens for the pupils to teach them horticultural skills. Brynglas school in Malpas had a very productive garden area.

These two happy gardeners were Sam Critchley and Trev Jones of the Gaer. They converted their lawns into potato patches.

The influx of American soldiers also affected many aspects of Newport life during this period, including their relationship with Newport women and girls. Many hearts were broken at this time but also many happy marriages were created.

The presence of Prisoners of War (POW) from Italy and Germany in Newport meant that their presence was seen on many farms and building projects. Some stayed in Newport after the war and made their homes with us in the town.

1940

The British and Worldwide Scene, Events and People

- Neville Chamberlain resigned as Prime Minister of Britain (1937-1940) and was succeeded by Winston Churchill, who became head of a coalition government on 11th May.
- Ernest Bevin joined the coalition cabinet of Prime Minister Winston Churchill as Minister of Labour and National Service; he was in charge of the mobilization of human and national resources throughout World War II (1939-1945).
- Churchill made a number of motivational speeches to Parliament and the public during the 1940s. 'I have nothing to offer but blood, toil, tears and

sweat', May 1940. 'We shall fight on the beaches, we shall fight on the landing grounds, we shall fight in the fields and in the streets, we shall fight in the hills; we shall never surrender', 4th June, 1940. 'Let us therefore brace ourselves to our duty, and so bear ourselves that, if the British Empire and its Commonwealth lasts for a thousand years, men will say, "This was their finest hour", 18th June, 1940. 'Never in the field of human conflict was so much owed by so many to so few', 20th August, 1940 about the Battle of Britain. 'Now this is not the end. It is not even the beginning of the end. But it is, perhaps, the end of the beginning', 1942 talking about the Battle for Egypt. 'From Stettin in the Baltic to Trieste in the Adriatic an Iron Curtain has descended across the Continent', 5th March, 1946. This was the first mention of the phrase 'Iron Curtain'.

- The Battle of Britain ended (June) with a British victory. 1,733 German planes were destroyed and 915 RAF planes lost. The 'Spitfires' and 'Hurricane' fighters out manoeuvred the German fighters. It was said that if Hitler only knew how short of replacement planes Britain was, the war of the air would have been won by Germany if the battle had continued another few weeks. It was about this time that the godly King George VI called for a day of prayer and thanksgiving for the country's preservation and need for continued protection. The churches were full for that event.

- Local Defence Volunteers (LDV) (later called the Home Guard), were formed as a makeshift anti-invasion forces. Initially their only weapons were sticks and home made wooden rifles for drill and manoeuvres. Many of their activities were aptly captured in the comedy series 'Dad's Army'. Anyone not 'called up' because they were in a vital war effort job, too ill or too old was expected to join the Home Guard. Farmers, coal miners, railway workers, nurses, etc. were in the vital category but some still volunteered to go into the forces.

- People, including children had to carry identity cards and gas masks. Drills were carried out in schools showing the way to the nearest shelters and how to best protect life if unable to reach them. This enlivened the imaginations of pupils and many 'war games' were played in the playgrounds.

- Evacuation of London children began as bombing of London intensified, many came to Newport and stayed with families.

Evacuee children with their name labels on their coats and their gas masks around their necks in bags or boxes. It was amazing how resilient the evacuee children were considering they were in a new environment and with new people and homes and lonely.

- British and French troops were evacuated from Dunkirk after an unsuccessful British invasion of France. Evacuation of British and French troops from Dunkirk lasted a few days, 27th May to 4th June. Many British troops were captured and sent to prisoner of war camps in Germany. Many did not return home as a consequence. There was an fleet of small boats sent to Dunkirk to rescue the retreating troops.
- The British troopship *Lancaster* was sunk by enemy bombing off St Nazaire and 2,500 crew and troops died.
- The first women workers on London's Underground started duty as ticket collectors and porters.
- The George Cross, the highest British civilian award for acts of courage, was instituted by the King.
- Coventry Cathedral destroyed by enemy bombing in November.
- London's Guildhall destroyed in an air raid and eight of Wren's churches (29th December).
- A 500 lb. bomb hit Broadcasting House in London killing several people. The newscaster paused for only a second and continued reading the news.
- Metal strips were introduced into Bank of England £1 notes as an anti-forgery device.
- Food rationing started in Britain and Ration Books were issued.

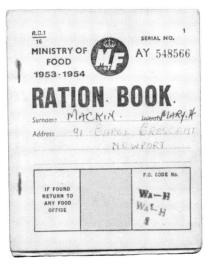

Food rationing started and ration books were issued to ensure a fair amount of sugar, bread, bacon and butter. Four ounces of butter could last a family of four for a week. Eight ounces of sugar were allowed. People started to have chicken sheds in their gardens to get fresh eggs and many gardens, front and back were dug up to make vegetable plots. Coupons were also needed for buying clothes. Before a garment could be purchased the necessary number of coupons had to be accumulated. The expertise and needlework skills of mothers meant that many garments of parents were often 'cut down' and the material re-used for smaller garments. The worn out section was cut out and the rest reused. Clothing coupons lasted into the 1950s.

- Leon Trotsky (1879-1940), the Russian revolutionary and once a leader, was attacked and assassinated in Coyoacan near Mexico City on 20th August, probably on the instructions of his arch rival Joseph Stalin.
- Ringo Starr (real name Richard Starkey) and John Lennon of the Beatles were born in Liverpool. Their music was considered to be revolutionary.
- Cliff Richard, the British entertainer was born in Lucknow, India as Harry Webb. He became a pop star.

World War events
- British troops arrive in Norway and Denmark for its invasion on 15th April and withdrew on 2nd May. Cliff Knight (one of the authors of this book) was at this scene and supported the troops with medical care as he was in the front line medical corps teams.
- Night bombing of Germany begins by RAF and Berlin attacked.
- The Italian fleet at Taranto, Italy was crippled by the Fleet Air Arm.
- London sustained severe damage by aerial bombing attacks during September.
- France capitulates and accepts the Armistice terms with Germany and the Vichy government was formed with Henry Pétain as head of state.
- Germany forces occupy the Channel Islands in July.
- Belgium King Leopold III surrendered to Germany and his country occupied.
- Japan signs a 10 year military and economic alliance with Nazi Germany and Italy.
- Japanese troops invade China on 23rd September.
- Holland, Belgium and Luxemburg invaded by Germans on 2nd May.
- HMS *Cossack* rescues about 300 British prisoners from German naval auxiliary ship *Altmark* in Norwegian waters on 16th February.
- The motor vehicle called the 'Jeep' was designed in USA for use in rugged terrain for troop and supply transportation.

The Local Scene, Events and People

Civic and Political
- Mayor was John Henry Swallow.
- Population of Newport 96,090.
- Rationing of one sort or another continued into the 1950s. Schoolchildren had their feet measured to see if they qualified for extra shoe coupons. Many children went to school with cotton wool in their socks to lengthen their feet size. One head teacher, the dreaded and often feared Miss Becker of the Gaer junior school, had a long piece of stick and poked people's toes to see if they were 'real'; she sometimes insisted pupils take off their socks if subterfuge was suspected.
- Because of coupons the school often supplied the 'daps' to wear for PE and dancing. One ex-pupil remembers, '... diving into a large pile of daps when they were tipped out hoping you could get a matched pair for size and different feet. Often you had to do PE without shoes or two left feet, it added to the hilarity of the exercises. There were often flying missiles of daps due to over enthusiastic activities. You were a hero if you could get a shoe through the open window. Daps were also used to smack bottoms as a means of discipline ... Wow that stung!'
- Dried egg powder was supplied, sometimes off ration, and it made excellent scrambled egg and was good in cooking.
- Food parcels were supplied by Australia for families and school children. In one school they were given out to classes who drew lots for its contents of dried fruit, sugar and tins of food. These parcels arrived periodically

throughout the war. It was a great day when it was announced that 'our school' had been selected to receive food parcels.

* Powdered chocolate was also supplied to schools and children were asked to bring jam jars. Many families mixed it with a little sugar and divided it out to be eaten as a 'sweet'. The children had little packets of it and dipped their fingers and licked it off. It lasted longer that way.
* Council turn down a recommendation to open cinemas on Sundays.
* It was reported that 336 men joined the LDV on the first day of recruitment.
* The main part of the Civic Centre opened.
* Newport Fighter Plane Fund raised £6,000 to help buy a 'Spitfire.'

Collections being made for the Spitfire Fund. The name of Newport was printed on the side of the Spitfire. Is that an airman in the background smoking a cigarette when in uniform in public?

* Responsible people were appointed as collectors in a street with the task of selling 'National Savings stamps'. Special projects were organized each year to boost the National Savings. The saving stamps could be redeemed for cash at the post office if required.
* 7,000 evacuee children arrived in the town, from London and the South East. They arrived in trains and the children were labelled. They were bussed around streets and 'displayed' to see who would take them in.

Commerce

* The Ordnance Factory in Corporation Road, opens. Engineering factories converted to Armament manufacture.
* Some poor children still benefit from the Mayor's 'Boot fund' which in 1940 raised £323 9s. 6d.

This photograph contains some of the staff of the Uskside Engineering Co. who made parts for tanks and other vehicles and armaments. The author's wife (Nancy Knight) is sitting on front of the tank (third from the right).

* Seven children from Newport were lost at sea, presumed drowned, when the steamship, SS *City of Benares* carrying 90 evacuee children from Britain to Canada was hit by a torpedo from a German submarine U48. Seventy-seven of the children died and 248 of the 406 adults.
* Clifford Montague Harris OBE made Chief Constable of Newport.

- W.H. Davies, the famous 'Tramp Poet' from Pill, died. If it had not been wartime more could have been made of a possible remembrance service, but it appears that not many people read the notice of his death in the *Argus*.
- The George medal was given to Detective Constable Charles Henry Cook for his heroic action when rescuing people after the bombing of the Alexandra Dock Hotel. The landlady was killed and several customers injured. Seven other people including civilians were awarded medals for bravery.

Far left: Charles Henry Cook (George Medal). Left: PC Edmund Wetter (OBE). Right: Joseph Draper (OBE). Far right: Harry Charles (Commended)

Far left: Frederick Keen (Commended). Left: C.A.H. Waters (OBE). Right: William Thomas Lewis (Commended) Far right: PC Emlyn Powell (Commended).

Places and Events

- A report said that Newport contained the most drunks in England and Wales.
- St Mary's Roman Catholic church, Stow Hill (*right*) celebrated its centenary.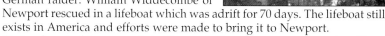
- Cleveland Oil Depot, Corporation Road, bombed. No fatalities.
- German plane crashes into 32 Stow Park Avenue. Three of the German crew die, pilot captured. Two residents of the house killed.
- Bombs fall on properties in Pottery Terrace, Baldwin Street, Capel Street, Lewis Street and Dewstow Street. Bomb fell on Dock Street and Caerleon tinplate works.
- The *Anglo Saxon* a merchant vessel which sailed from Newport in July sunk by a German raider. William Widdecombe of Newport rescued in a lifeboat which was adrift for 70 days. The lifeboat still exists in America and efforts were made to bring it to Newport.
- First nylon stockings on sale in Newport. They were very expensive. There was a big debate to say if it was more fashionable to have 'seamed' or 'non-seamed' stockings. It was reported that some ladies bought the cheaper non-seamed stockings and painted a black line on their legs to look like a seam.

Health

- Measles was widespread in Newport and also a few cases of Diphtheria; the isolation hospital in All-ty-yn was in constant use.
- The Lydia Beynon Maternity Hospital finally opened at the Coldra. The opening was delayed due to drainage difficulties.

1941

The British and Worldwide Scene, Events and People

- Britain's first jet-propelled aircraft, designed by Frank Whittle, flew for the first time in Cranwell.
- Nylon was made for the first time in Britain in Coventry for parachutes.
- Robert Baden-Powell died aged 83. He was a hero of the Boer War and founder of the Boy Scouts.
- Amy Johnson, from Hull was the first woman to fly solo from Britain to Australia in 1930. She was drowned in a mysterious accident on 5th January when she bailed out over the Thames estuary in bad weather when transporting a plane from one airport to another. She worked for the Air Transport Auxiliary.

World War events in Europe

- Bardia in Italy was taken by German troops on 5th January but retaken by British on 25th November.
- Tobruk in Libya captured by British and Allied forces on 5th January.
- Benghazi (North Africa) was captured by Germans on 7th February.
- Mogadishu, capital of Italian Somaliland was occupied by German troops on 26th February.
- British troops raid Lofoten off Norway on 4th March.
- Rommel opens his attacks in North Africa, 30th March.
- The Rock of Gibraltar, a key base and refuelling base was constantly bombarded by German planes. The caves deep into the rock were extensively used for storage and shelters.
- Belgrade occupied by German forces 11th April.
- Athens captured by Germans 27th April.
- Greece and Yugoslavia was invaded by Germans on 6th April and Greece was evacuated of troops on 2nd May.
- Rudolf Hess, a German Nazi leader and Hitler's deputy, was parachuted into Scotland on 10th May hoping to negotiate a peace agreement and imprisoned for some time in Abergavenny. He was tried in the Nuremberg War trials and sentenced to life imprisonment in Spandau prison where he was eventually the sole prisoner. He committed suicide in 1987.
- Battle cruiser HMS *Hood* was sunk on 24th May by the German Battleship *Bismark* 13 miles off the coast of Greenland and only three of the 142 crew survived.
- Battleship *Bismark* was sunk by the British ships HMS *Prince of Wales*, HMS *King George V* and HMS *Rodney* after a torpedo attack by 'Swordfish' planes from the aircraft carrier HMS *Ark Royal* on 27th May.

HMS *Rodney and other ships of the British fleet. The Rodney took a major role in the sinking of the battleship the Bismark.*

Ark Royal prior to the attack on the Bismark. It was sunk later on 14th November by a torpedo from a German U boat. One member of the crew was killed. HMS Legion picked up 1,487 survivors.

- Crete was invaded by German paratroopers on 20th May and British troops withdrew on 27th May.
- British and Russian troops enter Persia (Iran) 25th August.
- Germany attacks Russia, 22nd June. Siege of Leningrad by German forces began. Attack on Moscow but was halted on 4th December.
- Part of the House of Commons was destroyed by an enemy bomb.

World War concerning Japan

- 360 Japanese planes attack the American Pacific fleet anchored at Pearl Harbour, Ohau, Hawaii on 7th December.
- The attack spurred the US into entering the war. American casualties were 2,403 dead and 1,178 wounded. 188 aircraft destroyed and five battleships, one minelayer, and three destroyers were sunk or severely damaged.

- Britain and America declare war on Japan.
- Japanese forces land in Malaya on 8th December.
- British battleship HMS *Repulse* and HMS *Prince of Wales* were sunk off Malaya by Japanese aircraft on 10th December.
- Hong Kong surrenders to Japan on 25th December.

The Local Scene, Events and People

Civic and Political

- Mayor was William James Rudd.

Commerce

- Many engineering works were converted to making armaments. Many women employed in the factories on machines and also in the ordnance factories filling shells, etc.
- Bakeries were experiencing a shortage of flour and the white breads were being replaced with a brown flour which some people thought more healthy as it was unbleached. Cake shops had few in the way of 'fancy' cakes. Sugar, imported from overseas was in short supply. Sugar beet growing in Britain was increased.
- Farms had 'Land Girls' working on them as many men went to serve in the forces. They had a brown uniform and did all the jobs the men had done. Without them food production would have markedly declined.
- Children and families and youth organizations were encouraged to collect

unwanted metal objects (e.g. saucepans, kettles, etc.) to melt down to make items for defence and armaments. Railings around public and private buildings were sawn off and sent for scrap.

Scrap metal collectors from streets, schools guides and scouts etc. Notice the metal objects being waved. Also present Richard Davies, Dan Rowe, Mrs Roberts (WVS).

People

ATC units were formed in some secondary schools including the Newport High Schools. Photograph of St Julian's HS unit, in need of a session of disciplined 'square bashing'. Billy Bryant was the teacher.

- The Air Training Corps, a junior branch of the RAF was formed. During wartime 14 ex-pupils received wartime decorations ranging from DSO to BEM and 24 were mentioned in despatches. Over 800 ex-pupils served in HM forces in World War II. Letters and cards were sent to all each year and special letters to those men in prisoner of war camps. (From 'Services newsletter 1945' of St Julian's Boys school.)
- Many men over 18 received their Calling Up papers for the forces and reported for medicals prior to doing 'square bashing' and training during 1940 and 1941.
- In Newport three boys each given four strokes of the birch for misbehaviour. This was said to be the last birching in Newport.
- Women bus conductors were employed; they were nicknamed 'Clippies'.

Places and Events
- 200 allotment garden plots rented out to help the occupiers for the 'Digging for Victory' initiative to help people grow crops to feed their families.
- Maindee cinema closed.
- 16 Charles Street becomes Newport's Education Offices.
- 'Twanky Dillo', an unofficial song once sung at a speech day in St Julian's Boys High School in late 1940s, caught the imagination of rugby teams and was sung with gusto on many buses to and from games. It was in fact an old traditional folk song of the 1800s or earlier.
- Newport Destroyer Fund was started and helped to buy a destroyer worth £750,000.

- Newport Secondary School, Stow Hill (also called the Municipal Secondary School and Higher Elementary School) moves to the new school called St Julian's High School at Heather Road on 30th June, 1941. Separate boys' and girls' schools.

The foundation stone was put down in 1939. It was used after partial completion using all the old furniture from Stow Hill. Because of the War it was only 'officially' opened' in 1946. The head teacher was Mr Atkinson and headmistress Miss Crowther. The Germans celebrated just prior to the move by dropping a few bombs nearby, a few windows were broken.

Health

- All the hospitals made preparations for emergencies including bombings and also for large numbers of casualties.

War matters

- Bombs were dropped on Fields Park Road, Ridgeway Avenue and Glasllwch Crescent: 23 dead and 24 injured; 560 properties damaged.
- Many homes with spare bedrooms were forced to have lodgers often from the armed forces who were working locally. A Lodgings Officer visited homes to get the details of the householders and then assign lodgers. The lodgings were often called their 'Digs'.
- On 1st July large parachuted land mines fell on Kensington Place, Beechwood Road, Archibald Street, Eveswell Street, and Woodland Road; 35 dead and 46 injured. This was Newport's worst Air Raid.
- Bombs dropped in Beaufort Road and Place, Badminton Road, St Paul's Vicarage, Palmyra Place, Park Square and Belle Vue Park. Properties damaged.
- Bomb exploded on Gaer railway tunnel and Belle Vue Park opposite Whitehead's works. Many homes lost windows and had other damage. The shock wave of the bomb blew one of the authors out of bed. He was about 5 years old at the time.

- Some properties were commandeered for wartime use and one such house in Fields Park Road was used for Air Force Command and its interior redesigned and signs erected on doors etc.

House belonging to the Ludlows in Fields Park Road still has interesting archive items belonging to its wartime use by RAF. It also had its windows blown out when a bomb landed nearby.

- On 7th October several bombs fell on Rogerstone leaving 130 homes severely damaged.
- During the year the Alexandra Dock had been bombed five times and Newport had 51 casualties and 159 injured compared with Swansea's 387 killed and 412 injured and Cardiff's 355 killed and 502 injured.
- Newport prepares for a possible German invasion and mock gas attack staged in the town to demonstrate its readiness.
- Children and people told to carry their gas masks everywhere they went. They were contained in cardboard boxes on strings or in cylindrical black tin containers.
- People were told to be diligent and not to talk about vital wartime information about gun emplacements, factory details, troop movements, etc.

Commerce

Engine drivers were given exemption from serving in the forces if they requested it as their services were essential in keeping industry and towns supplied with goods. No. 6710 was used for shunting at Newport Docks

- The trains had to keep running to bring coal and steel from the valleys to the factories in Newport and other areas.
- A most unusual ship made of concrete was constructed at Jack's Pill shipyard.

- Vans belonging to firms around Newport were commandeered for wartime use.

Petrol was in short supply and only 'essential' journeys were allowed. Special petrol coupons were issued, also the petrol for forces and essential users contained a red dye to try to prevent illegal use of private cars with the 'black market' petrol. These and other vehicles could be 'called up' for transporting military goods if so required. Photograph supplied by John Bailey.

1942

The British and Worldwide Scene, Events and People

World War Two in Europe

* RAF made its first daylight bombing raid on the Ruhr (16th January) using Lancaster bombers and other planes.
* The island of Malta was awarded the George Cross (15th April) for its bravery and heroism during the heavy German and Italian bombardment. The convoy of supplies were under constant attack and as few as one ship in three arrived safely with supplies.
* Over 1,000 bombers raided Cologne (May).
* British Commandoes make a daring raid on the French Port of St Nazaire.
* Big battle at El Alamein prevented the German and Italian forces advancing into Egypt. An RAF Maintenance Unit was set up in Tura, 14 miles south of Cairo to maintain aircraft engines and repairs. This was one of a few in the area. The unit was called 111MU. It was located in deep caves lent by the Egyptian Ministry of Antiquities. The Germans bombed the yards many times in an endeavour to knock it out but did not succeed as most of the equipment was inside the deep caves.
* British and Canadian commandos raided the French port of Dieppe in Normandy.
* The Duke of Kent, son of King George V, and brother of King George VI, was killed in active service on 25th August.
* The forces led by Field Marshal Montgomery sent the German army led by General Rommel (called the 'Desert Fox') into full retreat starting at El Alamein and taking 9,000 German prisoners and destroying 300 tanks (November).
* The 'Spitfire' plane named *Pride of Newport* flew some missions.
* Tobruk, North Africa, captured by German forces on 20th June.
* American troops make a landing on the shallow beach of Oran (Algeria) on 8th-12th November.

The photos were taken at the time by American forces and copies swapped or sold to British troops. These were collected by Bill Howell.

- German advance into Russia was halted at Stalingrad (September). Russians counter-attacked and surrounded the German forces.
- On 3rd October the Germans made a successful launch of their 'V2' rockets and these were the first rockets and man made objects to be projected into inner space.
- The French Fleet in the harbour of Toulon was scuttled to prevent the advancing German army using them (November).

World War Two with Japan
- Manila (Philippines) overrun by Japanese forces (2nd January).
- Japanese forces invaded Burma and land in New Guinea and the Solomon Islands, (29th January). Later, American forces invaded and landed in the Solomon Islands.
- British naval base in Singapore surrendered to Japanese forces and Singapore surrenders on 15th February.
- Java surrenders to Japanese forces (9th March).
- Japanese bomb the Australian city of Darwin.

Other Events
- Gilbert Murray started the OXFAM charity.
- The British cruiser *Curacao* sunk off the coast of Donegal, Ireland, with the loss of 338 lives after a collision with the Cunard liner *Queen Mary*.
- The Beveridge Report on social issues was presented. This report formed the basis of the Welfare State benefits in Britain when later introduced.
- The pilot of an experimental jet fighter plane became the first pilot to leave the plane using an emergency ejector seat.
- 'Desert Island Discs' the BBC radio programme started and was presented by its creator Roy Plumley. It is still a popular programme today.
- Alan Turing invented the first 'programmable computer'. Alan Turing (1912-1954), took part in the 1948 Olympic games in the marathon where he did a time of 2 h 46 m. He was most well-known for his work on developing a mechanical machine that cracked the secret wartime codes of the Germans which he later developed into what we now call a computer system. He was awarded an OBE in 1945 for his war work. He committed suicide by eating an apple laced with cyanide probably due to the pressures of the then illegal side of his life as a homosexual.
- The Church of England relaxed its rule that all women must wear hats in church.
- In the University of Chicago the first controlled nuclear fission reaction was performed by a team led by Enrico Fermi (1901-1954) in December 1942. He later opposed the development of the hydrogen bomb on ethical grounds. He was born in Italy but moved to USA just before World War II due to the anti-Semetic feelings in Italy as his wife was Jewish. He died of cancer in 1954 probably brought on by his research with radioactive materials.
- Joe Louis (1914-1981) took the World Heavyweight boxing title for the 20th time. He defended the title 25 times before he fully retired in 1949.

The Local Scene, Events and People

Civic and Political
- The Mayor was George Scott.
- Opening of cinemas on Sundays again refused by the council.
- Soaps, sweets and chocolate join the wartime ration list.
- Ernest Bevin MP (Minister of Labour and National Services) opens the Merchant Navy Club at the junction of Commercial Road and Frederick Street, Pill. Later called the British Sailors Society HQ.

Commerce
- Many munitions factories employ large numbers of women and crèches were in place to care for the children.

People
- Death was reported of A.A. Newman, Town Clerk for 42 years and a Freeman of the Borough.
- Death of Kyrle Fletcher, noted Newport historian and writer. He contributed many articles in journals and newspapers on the history of the Newport area.
- David Watkins was born, one of the most exciting outside halves ever to play for Newport RFC. He played for Newport over 200 times and captained the team three times. In 1967 he turned professional for Salford but later returned to Newport and became Chairman of Newport Athletic Club.

Places and Events
- The Empire Theatre, Charles Street (also called the New Theatre) burned down.
- The Newport Postmaster in the *Argus* predicts that one day people would be able to talk to each other on telephones carried in their pockets … It seemed too far fetched to believe.
- Dancing introduced in Beechwood and Belle Vue Parks around the band stands. Ballroom dancing was also very popular and there were many halls throughout the town.
- Shortage of beer and other alcoholic drinks because of wartime leads to public houses restricting their hours of opening and resulting in much less drunkenness.
- Slight relaxation in total 'Blackout' restrictions. This was a great help to mobility at evening or night time. Motor cars, buses, lorries, motor cycle and bike headlights all had hoods on them which directed the beam through slits more towards the ground. The few street lights of low wattage also had hoods to direct the light to the ground and prevent any upward lighting effects which could direct enemy planes to targets. Air raid wardens had the favourite phrase of 'Put that light out' if they saw any stray light peeping around the thick blackout curtains of houses or offices.

- Some houses had thick 'black blackout curtains' others had internal shutters of hardboard over their windows as this not only kept the light out but also gave some protection should a window be shattered by a bomb blast. It also helped to keep heat in and in the summer kept rooms cool.
- There were definitely no shop window lights, but when the restriction was eased some went into town 'just to see the lights again'. It was a boost for morale as a possible indication that the war was coming to an end. It would be a few years before total restrictions were lifted.
- A popular song of that era was entitled 'When the lights go on again'.

1943

The British and Worldwide Scene, Events and People

World War events in Europe
- The Mohne, Eder and Sorde Dams in Germany were breached by 19 Lancaster Bombers of the 617 Squadron led by Guy Gibson on 16th May, using specially-designed cylinder-shaped bombs that bounced along the surface of the water. They were invented by Dr Barnes Wallis. The squadron was called the 'Dam Busters' after this event.
- The Allied troops invaded Sicily and captured the Island during July and August. Cliff Knight was there as a soldier in the medical corps.
- Benito Mussolini resigns as dictator of Italy and the Fascist regime abolished, 25th July.
- Leningrad was relieved on 18th January, having been besieged by the Germans for 16 months.
- Remnants of the German army outside Stalingrad surrendered, 31st January.
- Kiev was taken from the Germans on 6th November.
- The US Air Force made its first bombing raid on Germany, 27th January.
- Allied forces land in Salerno in Southern Italy. The Italian mainland was invaded on 3rd September.
- Germans seize Rome on 10th September.
- British and American troops land near Naples, 9th September and Naples taken on 1st October.
- Italy surrenders.
- The German battleship *Tirpitz* was severely damaged on 23rd September.
- The German battleship *Scharnhorst* was sunk off North Cape of France on 26th December.
- British troops capture Tripoli , 23rd January.
- Tunis and Bizerta in North Africa were captured by Allied troops on 7th May.

World War with Japan
- Salamaua (New Guinea) was captured from the Japanese on 14th September.
- Guadalcanal Island in the Pacific Ocean was cleared of Japanese forces 9th February.

Other Events
- British Government announced that income tax as a 'pay as you earn' (PAYE) scheme would come into effect in April 1944.
- A London tube train disaster killed 173 people on 5th March.
- The Nuffield Foundation for research was established in London.
- The government announced that to save coloured dyes all school uniforms would be either blue or grey.
- Men between 18-25 were be directed to the mining industry by ballot (2nd December).
- Battle of Britain Thanksgiving Service held in St Paul's Cathedral, London in May. King George VI urged the nation to pray for success and peace.

The Local Scene, Events and People

Civic and Political
- Mayor was Harry Godfrey Barker.
- King George VI, the Queen and Princess Elizabeth visited Newport on 29th March. They visited the works that contributed so much to the war effort.
- The Council refused by one vote the opening of cinemas on Sundays.

People
- Mr G.A. Coes, one of the original Transporter Bridge drivers, retired after 37 years of service. He and his wife were members of Alma Street Baptist Church.
- Group Captain Bailey received a severe reprimand and a fine for flying his plane under the span of the Transporter Bridge without permission.
- Clifford Montague Harris OBE was made Chief Constable of Newport.
- Some Prisoners of War were held in Newport. There were many POW camps around Newport and a large camp for Italian POWs was situated on the main Cardiff Road where Wyevale Garden Centre is now situated. The prisoners cultivated the land well for the future owners!
- In one area of Newport during the dark blackout nights there were rumours of the exploits of 'Dapper Dan'. He wore dappers (plimsolls) to creep up on unsuspecting females in the dark and 'pinch their bottoms and worse'. The call of 'look out here comes "Dapper Dan"' put fear into many children's hearts and was often called out in jest by boys playing in the streets.

Places and Events
- The *South Wales Argus* expands its High Street premises into Market Street.
- The local United States Servicemen's headquarters was established at Malpas Court.
- The ack-ack guns practised their skills by first shooting up a shell containing a series of parachutes released when they explode. The gunners tried to shoot them down. They did this over the lighthouse area of the sea. Any slightly damaged parachutes (which were made of silk or synthetic

material) would fall into the sea and some got washed in with the tide. Enterprising young lads gathered these red or white parachutes and sold them to ladies for 6*d*. or a shilling (if undamaged) for making into underwear and clothing. No coupons needed for these!

- There were guns and range finder encampments all around Newport along with barrage balloons. There was a camp called the Great Oak in Rogerstone (what is now Ruskin Avenue) and was built to house the 612 Regiment of the Royal Artillery. It had four guns of 3.7 in. diameter. This was one of the sites dotted around Newport. When the guns were fired the windows of nearby houses rattled. Another unit was located on Gaer Road.

Health
- Spread of venereal disease (VD) was worrying, American servicemen stationed in Newport were blamed. A special treatment clinic was set up for any unfortunate young ladies and men who thought they had been infected. Contraceptives were not in common usage and not easily purchased, although the USA forces seem to have had them. There was a special VD clinic set up in the Royal Gwent Hospital.
- The Chapel at the Royal Gwent Hospital was donated by Mrs C.H. Bailey, in memory of her husband C.H. Bailey the shipping magnate.
- Orthopaedic Unit opened at the Royal Gwent Hospital, the cost was £51,000.

The Fracture and Orthopaedic Unit at the Royal Gwent Hospital in 1943. Many a child left this unit with plaster on their arms or legs only to be 'signed' or drawn on at school. Some children even kept their casts as souvenirs!

1944

The British and Worldwide Scene, Events and People

- The Butler Education Act of Parliament raised the school leaving age to 15 and also demanded that schools have a daily collective Christian religious service.
- The types of secondary education available at this time were, the Grammar School for those who passed the 11+ exam, the Secondary Modern for those who passed but not quite as well, the Secondary Tech for the technically minded (starting at age 13), the non-selective secondary for the 11+ failures or those who couldn't afford to go to the high schools, etc. There were a number of bright pupils in this latter category who became pillars of Newport society. One such school in Maesglas was the school attended by Dick Richardson, later to become the European Heavyweight boxing Champion.
- Aneurin Bevan (1897-1960), British politician, born in Tredegar, Wales, was elected to the executive committee of the Labour party.

- Sir Henry Wood, English musical conductor and founder of the Promenade Concerts in 1895, died.
- Princess Elizabeth convinced her father that she be allowed into doing something for the war effort so she joined the Woman's Auxiliary Territorial Service where she was known as No. 230873 Second Subaltern Elizabeth Windsor. She became a driver and freely mixed with other members and was trained in mechanics and driving skills for her tasks. She was the only female member of the Royal family who had served in the forces during wartime up to that time.

World War Two events in Europe
- It was reported that 50 Allied forces officers were shot after escaping from a German prisoner of war camp.
- Monte Cassino in Italy was destroyed by bombers on 15th March and later captured by ground forces.
- Allied forces landed on the coast of Normandy on 6th June. The operation was called 'Operation Overlord' and 4,000 ships were involved. The invasion was also called D-Day.
- Paris was liberated by the Allies in August having been captured on 14th June, 1940.
- Allied forces landed at Anzio in Italy on 22nd June. Cliff Knight was a soldier at this landing.

One of the many landing crafts used in the invasions during 1944. Taken by a serving soldier at the landing.

- Allied forces liberated Rome, June.
- An assassination attempt on Hitler's life was made by a German staff officer, Claus Schenk Graf von Stauffenberg on 20th July.
- Allied forces landed in Southern France on 15th August and met little opposition.
- The British Airborne invasion of Arnhem and Eindhoven in Netherlands took place on 17th September using parachuted troops and gliders towed to the area by planes. The operation was called 'Market Garden' and involved the 1st British Airborne division and a Polish 1st Independent Parachute brigade. Their objective was to secure the bridge at Arnhem but they were unable to secure it due to stiff resistance and they had to withdraw by 26th September.
- Antwerp and Brussels were taken by the Allied troops. Holland entered.
- Cease fire declared in Finland (September).
- Bulgaria asks for Armistice (September).
- German General Rommel (1891-1944) called the 'Desert Fox' after his brilliant tactics at El Alamein, died by taking a cyanide pill before he could be arrested for taking part in a plot to kill Hitler. He died on 14th October, 1944.

US 'Flying Fortresses' started day time bombing raids.

- From bases in Britain US bombers began daytime bombing of Germany.
- 'Pluto' ('Pipeline under the ocean') across the English Channel supplied the Allied forces with fuel. It went from Shanklin, Isle of Wight. Some of the parts were manufactured in Newport.
- First flying bombs fell on England.
- Glen Miller, the popular American dance band leader was lost, presumed dead, in an aircraft accident over English Channel, 15th December.
- The Warsaw rising by its inhabitants was crushed by occupying German forces (3rd October).
- Athens liberated by Allied forces (14th October).
- The 'Battle of the Bulge' began in the Ardennes but met a violent counter attack by 15 German divisions on 16th December.
- Britain's largest and last battleship, HMS *Vanguard*, was launched at Clydebank in Scotland.

World War involving Japan
- American forces land on the Marshall Islands in the Pacific, 1st February.
- Orde Wingate, the British commander who led a group called the Wingate Raiders composed of commandos from the British, Burmese and Ghurkhas, was killed in April in a plane crash in the jungle in Assam.
- The Japanese fleet was crushingly defeated in World War II's largest naval battle at Leyte Gulf, Philippines. It involved 231 ships and 1,996 aircraft on 20th October.

Other Events
- Mount Vesuvius, near Naples, Italy erupted in February. Vesuvius was the volcano that in 79AD wiped out Naples and killed most of the people of Pompeii and left the city covered with dust and volcanic ash many feet deep.
- Franklin Roosevelt was re-elected American President for the fourth and record time.

The Local Scene, Events and People

Civic and Political
- The Mayor was George W. Armstead.
- Council vote again 'No ' to Sunday opening of cinemas.
- People flock to Belle Vue Park for the entertainment put on during the 'Holiday at Home' week organized by the council. This was because there were travel restrictions and also a shortage of fuel for non-military use.

Commerce
- In June Newport was preparing for the invasion of Normandy. The docks were full of vessels. Tree-lined roads and side streets including Forge Lane were full of tanks, lorries, armoured cars, etc. Newport factories had prepared some of the war materials. Whitehead's Iron and Steel Co. of Pill had provided steel for the 'Mulberry Harbour' and the 'Pluto' fuel pipe line and Lysaghts had provided much of the materials for tanks, guns and planes. The Royal Ordnance factory also played its part by filling bombs, shells and bullets with explosives. Newport was relatively lightly bombed as compared with Cardiff, Swansea and Bristol.
- The Newport Docks mainly did its loading at night and the ships arrived and left Newport under the cover of darkness and were down the Channel off Swansea by morning, hence Swansea was heavily bombed as the Germans seemed to believe the ships were being loaded from Swansea.

People
- Death of John Moxon, an alderman and highly respected citizen. He was born in 1864.
- Some evacuee children return to their homes from Newport families. Many lasting friendships were made.
- Joe Louis, world heavyweight boxing champion, gave an exhibition fight at the Newport Athletic grounds, Rodney Parade on 30th June, 1944. He was billed on the programme as Staff Sergeant Joe Louis Barrow (World Heavyweight Champion) and he fought Master Sergeant Keen Simmons (heavyweight champion of Virginia and Illinois). It was organized by the Monmouthshire County Military and Air Force Welfare Committee.

Places and Events
- Some street lighting was switched on and the downward pointing shades were removed and blackout restrictions eased for homes. No more shouts of 'Put that Light Out' from the police and air raid wardens.
- King George VI at Buckingham Palace posthumously awarded a VC to the late John 'Tubby' Linton for his bravery as a submarine captain. The presentation was made to his 14-year-old son William. 'Tubby' commanded a submarine *Pandora*; working on sinking Italian supply ships. He received a DSC in 1941. He then commanded the *Turbulent* and sunk more German and Italian supply ships to Rommel in North Africa, for

The rather innocuous monument to one of Newport's war heroes on the riverside near the 'Wave' sculpture and Theatre Centre.

which he received the DSO. His submarine was eagerly hunted by German submarines but he skilfully evaded them. His submarine was sunk by a mine off Corsica and he and 66 crew died. For his own and his crew's bravery he received the Victoria Cross. In 1987 a memorial was unveiled on the banks of the Usk. William (Tubby's son) also entered the submarine naval unit six years later as a sub-lieutenant and as a member of HM Submarine *Affray*. Unfortunately he died when the submarine failed to surface in the English Channel on 16th April, 1951, it carried 75 submariners. Tubby Linton was born in Malpas. There is a pub in the town centre named after him.

- Electricity and Transport department of the town council split into two separate departments.
- Stow Hill Baptist Church for sale. Established 1860.
- Extensive fire at Newport High School, a grammar school, Queen's Hill. It was thought it started in the Chemistry laboratory.

- Home Guard begins to stand down (the 2nd Mon (Newport) Battalion are shown above).

Health
- Many wounded British and German servicemen treated at the Royal Gwent Hospital and St Woolos Hospital. Children from other parts of Britain brought to Newport because of the danger caused by 'V1' and 'V2' rocket bombs' in London and the South Coast areas.
- In the book about the Royal Gwent Hospital (by Brian Peeling *see Bibliography*) it quotes from the records book: '… June 1944 - British and German soldiers wounded in the invasion of the Normandy Beaches arrive at the Royal Gwent Hospital. Some soldiers said to be arrogant and as young as 15'.

1945

The British and Worldwide Scene, Events and People

World War Two events in Europe
- Fighting in Athens ended on 5th January.
- Russian Red Army occupy Budapest on 13th January.
- Russian Red army enter Auschwitz, Poland, on 27th Janaury. It was a Nazi concentration camp used to exterminate Jews and other political prisoners and social minorities. Over two million people are estimated to have been exterminated there.
- Russian Red Army occupy Warsaw on 27th January.
- Dresden in Germany, at one time famous for its architecture, was flattened by bombing killing 135,000 people and destroying 80 per cent of the city. 1,400 RAF planes and 45 American planes took part.
- Heinrich Himmler, chief of the SS and Gestapo was arrested in April but committed suicide shortly afterwards.
- Joseph Goebbels, the Nazi leader, committed suicide in Hitler's bunker in Berlin after killing his wife and six children just as the Allied troops were entering Berlin.
- Russians took Berlin on 2nd May.
- Channel Islands liberated in May.
- German and Italian armies in Italy surrendered on 29th April.
- Hitler and his wife Eva Braun committed suicide in his bunker beneath the Chancellery in Berlin on 30th April.
- The concentration camps were liberated. In total approximately six million inmates had been exterminated in them, the majority were Jews.
- Vidkun Quisling, the puppet premier of Norway during the war, was executed by a firing squad in Oslo on 24th October. His name has become used as a name for traitor.
- Pierre Laval (Prime Minister of the Vichy Government from 1942 to 1944) collaborated with the Germans and was executed for treason.
- The Nuremberg War Tribunal began with the trials of 24 Nazi leaders.
- Russian and US armies link up in Germany on 27th April.
- Allies take Cologne on 6th March.
- Anne Frank, the famous child diarist, (1933-45) died.

- Mussolini the Italian dictator and fascist and his mistress Claretta Petacci were killed by Italian partisan fighters on 28th April.
- German forces in Germany, Holland and Denmark surrendered on 4th May, World War II ended on 8th May called Victory in Europe Day or VE day.

World War Two events involving Japan
- US troops landed in Luzon (Horn of the Philippines) on 9th January.
- Burma road to China re-opened on 28th January.
- US troops landed on the Japanese island of Iwo Jima on 19th February. It was a strategic base from which to attack the Japanese mainland. Heavy fighting occurred and 6,000 US troops lost their lives and 20,000 Japanese died. The battle ended in March.
- US troops invaded Okinawa, a Japanese island in April and air attacks on Japanese mainland 28th May.
- On 6th August the first atomic bomb ever to be released in warfare fell over Hiroshima and 129,558 people were killed or injured and 176,987 made homeless. Sixty per cent of the city was destroyed and an area of 10 square kilometres was devastated. 343,698 people once lived in the city.
- On 9th August one-third of the city of Nagasaki was destroyed by an atomic bomb in an endeavour to force the Japanese to surrender. 66,000 people were killed or injured. One Newport soldier who visited the site some months later when the radiation levels were dissipated claimed that he 'saw nothing but complete flattened buildings and devastation in an area larger than from St Mellons to Caerwent and equally as wide: "I'll never forget it"'.
- Rangoon, capital of Burma was taken from the Japanese by British troops.
- Allies re-occupy Singapore also Hong Kong after defeating the Japanese.
- Unconditional surrender by Japan on 14th August, 'Victory over Japan Day' or VJ day was celebrated on 15th August with street parties and further parties when the prisoners of war returned to their homes. Many returned home emaciated and weak and some were left with medical and health conditions that affected the rest of their lives.

Other Events
- The Yalta Conference between President Roosevelt, Winston Churchill and Stalin made a declaration on 11th February that agreed to ensure that Germany would never again be a military threat to the world and worked out the post-war strategy of bringing the Nazi criminals to justice.
- USA President Roosevelt died on 12th April. He had polio and was wheelchair bound all through the war.
- Potsdam conference on 31st July between USA, Britain and USSR decided the political and economic principles governing the treatment of post-war Germany.
- A world security charter was established at a conference in San Fransisco to create the United Nations on 16th July. The League of Nations was dissolved.
- Yugoslavia was proclaimed a Communist Republic under the dictatorship of Tito (1892-1980).
- The Louvre Museum in Paris was reopened.
- School leaving age in Britain raised to 15.

R.A.F. Form 2520/25

RELEASE AUTHORISATION

PART I

To be completed in Unit except when marked**.

Rank L.A.C.   Number 1277351

Initials T.   Surname JONES

Release of the above-named airman is hereby authorised as a Class A release, and he is relegated to Class G.I. of the Reserve.
The effective date of release (i.e. last day of service) is   29.11.45 **.

To be completed at the Dispersal Centre

It is hereby certified that the above airman served in the R.A.F. on whole-time service during the following periods:

From

11.3.41   S.WA. 70

2.10.45
4.10.45.

(Date of departure from Dispersal Centre)

He is granted 56 days' leave on release commencing the day following the date of departure from the Dispersal Centre.

R.A.F. Form 2520/25
(continued)

RELEASE AUTHORISATION
(continued)

PART II

Instructions to Class B releases to report for Employment
You have been released to take up employment

as a _____ (M. of L. code number _____).

Delete one of these

and are to report within seven days from your departure from this Dispersal Centre to the following Employment Exchange _____

OR

with Messrs. _____

of _____ to whom you are to report within seven days from your departure from this Dispersal Centre.

You will ordinarily be required to commence work on the expiration of your leave, but you may if you desire commence at any earlier time.

PART III

Date   4.10.45.

[stamp: No. 101 PERSONNEL DISPERSAL CENTRE RECORD OFFICE DETACHMENT ROYAL AIR FORCE -2 OCT 1945]

for A.O. i/c Records

R.A.F. FORM 2783

NOTIFICATION OF FINAL PAYMENT OF PAY AND ALLOWANCES AND AMOUNT DUE FOR WAR GRATUITY AND POST WAR CREDIT.

Class A and C Releases—Other Ranks.

TO

1277351. LAC. Jones S.
31, Lyndhurst Cir,
Newport
Mon.

Postal drafts to the value of £ 7 : 9 s. 1 d. are enclosed in final settlement of your pay account, including leave rate of ration allowance, up to and including 29.11.45 which is the last day of your release leave.

*This payment includes the sum of £ _____ payable for Service Gratuity (ex regular airmen only) or for the award of the following decoration(s) or medal(s) _____

In addition you are entitled to a payment for War Gratuity and Post War Credit. Payment will be made into a Post Office Savings Bank Account to be opened in your name, and the amount will be credited to the account on the 57th day after you leave the Dispersal Centre. A Post Office Savings Bank book will be dispatched to reach you as near to the 57th day as possible. The book will be forwarded to the address shown above. It is therefore important that you notify any change of address prior to the receipt of this book, to the Director, Post Office Savings Bank, Blythe Road, West Kensington, W.14., quoting your service number, rank and name (in block letters) and the particulars of your Savings Bank Account as follows:— *Fold here*

Account Particulars

K.15.17366

For your information your entitlement to War Gratuity and Post War Credit is as follows:—

War Gratuity

	£	s.	d.
For rank of A.C.			
54 months @ 10/- per month	27		
Post War Credit			
1429 days @ -/6 per day	35	14	6
TOTAL £	62	16	6

Please turn over

Two documents that every serviceman longed for … release papers and the end of the war. Included is one such set of papers from an ordinary serviceman who received £62 14s. 6d. for his four and a half years service in the RAF. More was paid if the servicemen served overseas for any length of time.

- In Britain the Labour party won a general election on 26th July and Clement Atlee was made Prime Minister.
- Atlee visited Newport.

Atlee and his wife visited Newport and here they meet Councillor Bill Moore.

- Aneurin Bevan (1897-1960), British political leader, born in Tredegar, Wales became Minister of Health (1945-51) in the Labour government of Prime Minister Clement Attlee. Bevan and was instrumental in establishing the National Health Service.
- Family allowance payments were first introduced in Britain and was five shillings per week for the second child and subsequent children. No payment was allowed for the first child.
- David Lloyd George died aged 82.
- Dr Fisher of London made Archbishop of Canterbury.
- Duke of Windsor resigns from the office of Governor of the Bahamas on 15th March.
- The first installation of fluorescent lighting in Britain on Piccadilly Circus Underground platform.
- British forces demobilised into 'civvy' life and were given a new set of clothing and a small financial gratuity, related to their war service. One soldier said, 'I had never had so much money in my pocket all at once, it was over £25. My new shoes were killing me and, myself and colleagues on the train from Harrogate to home, all looked like 'Taylor's Dummies' in appallingly fitting new suits in garish colours. We were all glad to get out of the forces and there was a sort of peculiar silence on the train as we left. Our memories were with the times when we wore the uniforms and had close colleagues some of whom did not reach the end of the war. We talked of what we were going to do after our few weeks leave was over and what were the job prospects. It was a new and changed world we were returning to. Some had jobs lined up while others had no trade or immediate job prospects but we all said "It will be OK, we have faced some bad times during the war, the future must be better than war". But would it be?'
- Air raid warnings were discontinued. The screaming, piercing sound of the air raid siren was only relieved when the 'all clear' siren was sounded. The sirens were located in every area of Newport and on hearing them people were urged to 'take shelter' for fear of an air raid. The air raid wardens would shout out 'Take cover' and direct people in town and other areas to shelters.
- George Orwell wrote *Animal Farm* which contained one well known phrase 'All animals are equal, but some animals are more equal than others'. He died in 1946 of TB aged 46.

CELEBRATIONS OF PEACE PROGRAMME

V. J. DAY WEDNESDAY, 15th AUGUST

3 p.m. **VICTORY PARADE.**
The Parade will assemble at the Cattle Market and will proceed along Commercial Road, Commercial Street, High Street, Newport Bridge, Rodney Road to the Athletic Grounds.

His Worship the Mayor (Councillor Geo. W. Armstead) and Brig. Gen. Joseph L. Philips, U.S. Army Commanding General, South Wales Ports, will take the salute at the Athletic Grounds.

4 p.m. **SERVICE OF THANKSGIVING** at the Athletic Grounds.

5 p.m. **VICTORY FETE AND GALA AT SHAFTESBURY PARK,** which His Worship the Mayor will officially open. Open until Midnight.

THE LARGEST FUN-FAIR NEWPORT HAS EVER SEEN. ATTRACTIONS.

COMPETITIONS. Valuable prizes will be given.
Bands. Sports. Orchestras.

REFRESHMENTS of all kinds will be available at the Park.
Admission : Adults 6d. Children 3d. *Service personnel in uniform and Pensioners (on production of Pension Book) admitted free.*

7.30 p.m. DANCING at Stow Hill Drill Hall until Midnight.

9 p.m. Flood-Lighting of St. Woolos Cathedral, the Civic Centre and Newport Castle.

9 p.m. **THE KING SPEAKS.** His Majesty's Speech will be relayed from the Town Hall.

9.30 p.m. DANCING outside the Town Hall.

10 p.m. **BONFIRE AND FIREWORKS** display at Shaftesbury Park.

65—Peace Celebration Programme August 1945

V. J. PLUS 1 DAY—THURSDAY, 16th AUGUS[

2 p.m. **FETE AND GALA** at Shaftesbury Park. Open u
Midnight.
Competitions, etc.

Admission : **Adults 6d.: Children 3d.** Ser
*personnel in uniform and Pensioners (on production
Pension Book) admitted free.*

7.30 p.m. **DANCING** at Stow Hill Drill Hall until midnig

8.30 p.m. **FLOOD-LIGHTING** of St. Woolos Cathedral t
Civic Centre and Newport Castle.

9.30 p.m. **DANCING** outside the Town Hall.

V. J. PLUS 2 DAY—FRIDAY, 17th AUGUST

CHILDREN'S DAY.

2 p.m. **AT SHAFTESBURY PARK.**
Special attractions. **Sports of all kinds.** Competitions.
Punch and Judy. Jeep Rides.
Special competitions for children—Dancing, Singing, etc.
Valuable Prizes given.

V. J. PLUS 3 DAY—SATURDAY, 18th AUGUST

2.30 p.m. **GRAND GYMKHANA: HORSE SHOW** and
GALLOWAY RACES. AT SHAFTESBURY PARK
Pony Races, Jumping, Children's Jumping Competitions.
Valuable prizes will be given.
(*See later announcement*).

SUNDAY AFTER V. J. DAY CELEBRATIONS
19th AUGUST

7 p.m. **AT ODEON CINEMA.** PEACE CELEBRATIONS
CONCERT including N.E.C.O. Orchestra, Guest Artists
and winners of the Fete and Gala Music Competitions.

Peace Celebrations and the Fete and Gala will continue on subsequent week-days. (*See later announcements*).

VE Day party in Alice Street.

The Local Scene, Events and People

Civic and Political

- The Mayor was Sarah Jane Hayward, the second lady Mayor (the first being Mrs Hart).
- Field Marshal Bernard Montgomery visits Newport.

Field Marshal Bernard Montgomery visited to receive the Freedom of the Borough on 29th September, 1945. He inspected the Army Cadets on parade outside the post office in the High Street. He also performed other local duties.

- VJ Day was also celebrated later in the year from the VE parties. It was a year of street parties on meagre rations but the inventiveness of the ladies made party tables look fit for a king. Similar street parties were held when a serviceman returned home.
- Civil Defence Force and Home Guards disbanded.
- Newport Corporation run the bus service between Newport and Cardiff jointly with Cardiff City Council.

People

- Death of James Walker MP for Newport in 1929. He was the first Labour MP in Newport.
- Death of Sir Reginald Clarry (Conservative) MP for Newport 1920-1930s.
- Petula Clark, the famous singer, appears at the Odeon cinema, Clarence Place, to complete the VE Day celebrations.
- Many 'Welcome Home' parties for the soldiers and lavish parties for the ex-prisoners of war.
- George (Twyber) Travers, famous rugby forward who played 25 times for Wales. He died at his home, 70 Lime Street on Boxing Day. Father, George, and son, William (Bunner) Travers, were both outstanding hookers for Newport and Wales and won 37 caps between them. George 25 (between 1903-1911) and William 12 (between 1937-49, the war obviously affected the number of caps he could have won).

Places and Events
- Tredegar Hall cinema, Stow Hill, closed.
- Peter Freeman (Labour) wins election to MP.
- Residents given the option of buying their Anderson air raid shelters for £40; many were used as garden sheds or allotment stores.
- The Alway estate started being built.
- On 26th August the heaviest rain fell on the town for 70 years.
- Temporary prefabricated bungalows were needed for forces returning and also the increased size of families due to the post-war 'baby boom'. The houses were erected in various locations.

Temporary prefabricated bungalows were erected in various locations and rented to residents. People became very attached to these residences. This was often the first house that the residents occupied as their own and many bought them when given a chance to do so. They were commonly known as 'Prefabs'. They were estimated to last for 10 years. The radio comedians of the era had many quips about the 'Prefabs' and Charlie Chester show had one set of sketches in which it was chanted 'Down in the jungle living in a tent, Better than a Prefab, No rent'.

The two-storey 'steel houses' were thought to have a life of more like 15 years but they are still in existence in 2007. Some have been redeveloped on the original plots and had brick and facings changed. They were relatively spacious houses. The 'tin' roof sometimes was a bit noisy when it rained hard! Estates of these steel houses were referred by some as 'Tin Town' but in later years the term was one of endearment not ridicule. The roof and upper storey shuttering was made of steel, the lower floor was rendered breeze blocks.

Health
- At the Preliminary Nurses Training School, it was suggested that males as well as females should train as nurses. This was met with apprehension by many both in the nursing profession and also the public
- By this time many long term wounded service men were recovering at the Royal Gwent and St Woolos Hospitals.

Things of Interest
- After the war the heavy blackout curtains were ingeniously converted into many garments because clothing material was scarce. Bleaching and dying made the black curtains into acceptable colours for clothing, cushion covers or curtains. Black football and PE shorts were common.

1946

The British and Worldwide Scene, Events and People

- Aneurin Bevan, proposes the National Health Service (NHS).
- Prime Minister Atlee introduced compulsory National Service on 12th November for men over 18.
- Anniversary of World War Victory Day was celebrated on 8th June.
- Churchill's famous 'Iron Curtain' speech, 5th March. 'From Stettin in the Baltic to Trieste in the Adriatic an iron curtain has descended across the continent'. It resulted in an invisible barrier between Russian-held territories and the rest of Europe.
- £281 million loan from Canada to Britain agreed 1st March.
- £937 million loan from USA to Britain agreed 13th March.
- National Coal Board was set up in UK on 7th March.
- Bread rationing began in UK.
- H.G. Wells (Herbert George Wells) the science fiction writer died on 12th August at the age of 79.
- Alistair Cooke the famous writer, columnist and broadcaster gave the first of many hundreds of 'Letters from America' programmes on BBC radio.
- George Best, the legendary Northern Ireland soccer player was born in Belfast.
- The first TV licences were issued in UK at a cost of £2.
- John Logie Baird, the Scottish inventor and pioneer of the development of television, died.
- 'Housewives' Choice' a record request programme started on BBC radio, it ran for decades.
- Stevenage in Hertfordshire became the first of many 'New Towns' designated in post-war Britain.
- The uses of microwaves were discovered by an American, Percy Spencer, almost by accident when using the strong magnets in Radar development.
- King David Hotel in Jerusalem was blown up on 22nd July as it was the British Headquarters. War between Britain and Palestine.
- The first ballpoint pen went on sale having been invented by the Hungarian László Biro. It was invented in 1938, patented in 1943 and came onto the British market in 1946. It is probably the most used invention of the century.
- America started further atomic bomb tests at Bikini Atoll on 30th June in an endeavour to find a way to harness the energy from an atomic explosion and use it for peaceful purposes like generating electricity. Coincidentally the 'Bikini' swimming costume was first modelled in Paris Fashion Show that same year.
- League of Nations wound up on 18th April.
- The General Assembly of the United Nations was opened in New York on 23rd October. Trygve Lie became the first United Nations Secretary General on 1st February (1946-1952).
- Nuremberg War Crime Trials carried out the execution of some leading Nazis including Von Ribbentrop, Rosenberg and Streicher on 16th October.

Goering committed suicide by poisoning himself a few hours before he was due to be hanged on 23rd October. The Nazi propagandist William Joyce, called 'Lord Haw Haw', was hanged for treason. He had broadcast in English from Germany many incorrect details of the war and how Britain ought to give in and how hopelessly they were doing. He held a British passport.

The Local Scene, Events and People

Civic and Political

- The Mayor was Reginald Silas Tyack.
- 17th January in Alexandra Docks saw the first unloading of bananas, probably the first banana seen in the town for six years. Some children had to be shown how to unpeel the banana as many thought you had to eat everything! Queues formed in shops to buy these bananas. In fact queues formed sometimes with people not knowing what they were queueing for, biscuits, white bread, coffee, tea, etc.
- Malpas Court once the home of Thomas Prothero, the Town Clerk and influential citizen, was left in ruins after its use by soldiers during the war. Later Newport Council bought Malpas Court.
- A full parade of United States servicemen marched to the Athletic grounds before leaving Newport for 'home'.
- Alma Street Baptist Church back premises which were used by USA troops were left in such a bad condition that they had to be knocked down. The 'long hall' was used as a rifle range.
- The Roll of Honour shows the following Newportonians who gave their lives during the war: Royal Navy, Merchant Navy, Royal Marines - 719, Army - 281, RAF - 155, Service unknown - 145, Total - 1,300.
- Bread rationing continued. World shortage of wheat, largest rations went to manual workers.
- Referendum on Sunday cinemas opening gives a 'Yes ' vote.
- The Corps of the South Wales Borderers (24th Foot) granted the Freedom of the Borough.
- Welsh Guards' victory march passes through Newport.

Commerce

- The Royal Ordnance factory, Corporation Road sold and became Standard Telephones and Cables Ltd.
- HMS *Enterprise* taken into Cashmore's, Pill, for scrapping after her glorious war career.
- Monsanto Chemicals Works move to Newport.
- Newport Council abolished tolls on the Transporter Bridge. 118,779 passengers crossed the Bridge during the year, also 40,690 cycles and 3,385 vehicles.

People
- Evan, the Baron and 2nd Viscount Tredegar, gives up his residence at Tredegar House, the ancestral home of the Morgan family and goes to live on his Surrey estate. He was experiencing financial difficulties and by the early part of 1950 he had to sell off everything including the famous 'Tredegar Silver'. Since the beginning of the 15th century, Tredegar House and estate was owned by the Morgans one of the great Welsh families. After the Civil War the present grand house was built. The family fortunes flourished down the generations, but greatly increased by the business enterprises of Sir Charles Gould Morgan throughout the 18th century. They owned the grounds around the dock area and charged a levy on every ton of coal crossing their lands. The Morgans and the various Lord Tredegars were generous to Newport by donating land for buildings, finances for the Hospital and they were well respected for the things they did for the citizens of Newport. It was a matter of great disappointment when the latter Lord Tredegar spent the family fortunes on profligate living and selling off the treasures of the estate, caused also by large death duties imposed by the State.

Places and Events
- Demolition of Communal Street Air Raid shelters begins. Their thick concrete construction meant a lot of hammering and noise. In many areas of the town the children lost one of their 'play areas'.
- St Joseph's Private Hospital opens at Harding Avenue, Malpas.
- Newport County play in the Second Division of the Football League.
- Council refuses to grant permission for the playing of games on Sundays in the parks.

1947

The British and Worldwide Scene, Events and People

- Princess Elizabeth married to Prince Philip Mountbatten in Westminster Abbey on 20th November. The BBC covered the event in 42 different languages. Crowds on the streets of London were 50 deep in places.
- Lord Mountbatten became Viceroy of India, 20th February. Britain was due to withdraw from India by June 1948.
- Coal mines were nationalised on 1st January to become the National Coal Board. It had been the committed Labour party policy since the 1920s that when they came into power they would nationalise the coal industry. Miners experience a five day week.
- Coal crisis in February due to extreme weather, snow and ice and there was an industrial power switch off.
- Great Britain endured the worst snow blizzards in February since 1894. The snow lasted on the ground into March. It disrupted road and rail services

An overnight snow fall in 1947. A little boy's dream ... no school, only playing in the snow. In some parts of Britain snow piled up into drifts up to 7m (23 ft) high in March. Blizzards reached wind speeds of more than 100 mph (160 km/h), the most violent snowstorms recorded in the UK. Transport and communications were greatly affected and many older people were isolated and were advised to stay in and wear as many clothes needed to keep warm and save fuel. Neighbours were good at looking out for people in difficulty. There was friendship in adversity, something fostered during the war.

and the country came to a standstill on a few occasions. Fuel was difficult to buy as the tips were frozen solid and many households were driven to burning unwanted objects, collecting wood and making coal bricks from coal dust and cement often mixed with shredded paper. Schools were closed for some time and even when opened the children were often taught in their overcoats.

- On 20th February the Dover to Ostend ferry service was suspended because of pack ice in the sea as temperatures plunged to minus 21C (-6F).
- That winter was also the longest on record in the UK without sunshine. This would seem to be the opposite to global warming.
- Food supplies ran short. A fifth of the national livestock died and winter crops were frozen into the ground.
- Bread was still rationed.
- Transport was crippled. Daily power cuts were brought in and traffic lights were switched off to save electricity.
- Industrial production fell by 25 per cent, unemployment doubled to four million people and exports were crippled.
- The Labour Government was forced to make big cuts in spending and sterling was devalued the following year.

- Flooding in Britain as the snow melted was the worst on record and millions of cattle drowned.
- Potato rationing began in UK from November.
- The fresh meat ration was reduced to one shillings worth a week.
- Government announced the banning of mid-week sport to try to boost industrial production.
- The FA Cup Final between Charlton Athletic and Burnley was the first to be televised from start to finish.
- Silver coinage was replaced with cupro-nickel alloy. The silver 6*d.* pieces etc. were worth more for their silver content than the currency value.
- Transistor radios were coming onto the market.
- Stanley Baldwin, three times British Conservative Prime Minister who later became Earl Baldwin of Bewdley, died.
- Britain imposed martial law in Palestine.
- The Marshall Plan (a programme of US aid to Europe) was inaugurated on 5th June. This was a plan to give financial aid to rebuild Europe, its agriculture, coal and industries. It ended in 1952 when it was felt that its aims had been completed.
- India including Pakistan become independent Nations on 15th August. The first Indian prime minister was Pundit Nehru.
- Howard Hughes in USA piloted the world's largest plane on its maiden flight.
- The first supersonic flight was achieved in California on 14th October.
- The Dead Sea Scrolls dated between 150 BC-68 AD were found in caves west of the River Jordan.

The Local Scene, Events and People

- Everyone remembers 1947 for its cold weather and extreme snow fall. Melting snow led to some flooding. As the thaw set in many houses had leaking pipes as the frozen water inside them had burst the pipes. Plumbers were in great demand.
- The summer of 1947 was ironically one of the warmest of the century up to that date. Was this year an example of global cooling or global warming? Many people blamed it on the atomic bomb experiments being done.

Civic and Political
- Mayor was Thomas F. Mooney (1947-49).

Commerce
- James Mahoney of Portland Street, Pill, the oldest scrap metal dealer in South Wales, celebrates its centenary.
- H. Lotery & Co. (Uniforms) come to Newport. Well-known makers of uniforms for the services, etc.

The Jones' shop was opposite Maindee police station on corner of Livingstone Place. First owned by Alf Jones then Trev and Edna Jones. The adverts were all sponsored by tobacco firms or sweet companies.

People
- Death of Jerry Shea at 56 Alma Street, famous rugby player, boxer and athlete.
- Death of Jonny Basham at 12 Mountjoy Street, European champion boxer.
- Highly respected and much-loved Revd David. W. Ingram, minister of Alexandra Road Baptist Church, retires after 23 years' service. Known as 'the Bishop of Pill'.

Places and Events
- Potatoes rationed due to harsh winter. Food shortages were becoming serious.
- Maindee Cottage Gospel Mission established at Probert Place.
- The Pavilion Cinema, Stow Hill, becomes a variety theatre.
- Pill Harriers RFC, the famous Newport sports club was wound up after 60 years.

Health
- Children often had 'chapped' legs and chilblained legs from wearing damp and rough clothing. Vaseline and Germoline was always the answer to these. To 'build you up' in cold weather children were dosed with cod liver oil, malt extract, Virol and Parishes food.
- There were many cases of hypothermia referred to the hospitals but many people could not get to the doctors or hospitals but everyone was encouraged to 'keep a look out for your elderly neighbour'. There were many heart rending stories told of these times both good and bad.
- The hot summer brought out many home made creams as an antidote for sun burn. There was not such a thing as sun cream. Calamine lotion was available and some children were covered in the pink/white lotion to 'take the heat out of the sun burn'.
- Smoking was still not condemned by the medical profession although many thought there was strong correlation between smoking and chest complaints and lung cancers. Smoking had become the norm during war time and the forces were issued with cheap cigarettes, this in many cases started the addiction.

1948

The British and Worldwide Scene, Events and People

- Prince Charles was born in November.
- The National Health Service came into being in July. There was a run on the dental service for free false teeth and on the opticians for new glasses.
- Electricity industry in UK was nationalised in April.
- Railways in UK nationalised in January.
- Bread rationing ends in UK.
- Corporal punishment was abolished in UK.
- Andrew Lloyd-Webber was born in London.

- Alcoholics Anonymous was founded in London having been in existence in America since 1935.
- The first full size supermarket in Britain was opened by the Co-op in London.
- The Olympic Games opened in London, the Winter Olympics were in St Moritz, Switzerland. It was the first Olympic Games since 1936. Starting blocks for sprinters were introduced for the first time.
- The first Morris 'Minor' rolled off the production line at Cowley, Oxford. The original models had a split windscreen and had a little arm-like illuminated indicators that shot out when turning. If you did not retract them before getting out of the car invariably you would knock into them and break them off. Flashing indicators were introduced later.
- The Royal family went to see Danny Kaye (USA) at the London Palladium. This was the first 'Non Command Performance' attended by any reigning British monarch.
- Harry Truman was elected US President in November.
- Orville Wright, the younger of the two brothers who pioneered aeroplane flights, died.
- Ceylon became a self-governing dominion within the Commonwealth (re-named Sri Lanka in 1972).
- Hideki Tojo the Japanese Premier who provoked the Americans to enter World War II by bombing Pearl Harbour and sinking much of the American fleet was hanged as a war criminal. Some areas in Newport burnt, on bonfire night, effigies.
- Mahatma Gandhi, the Indian political leader was assassinated in Delhi in January in his own garden by a Hindu extremist. He was an ardent Hindu and exerted political pressure by going on hunger strikes.
- North Korea becomes independent and becomes a republic with Syngman Rhee as its first President.
- Berlin Airlift starts in July to supply food and goods to West Berlin as it was surrounded by the Russians in the East German communist state.
- New state of Israel proclaimed in May as the British mandate in Palestine ended.

The Local Scene, Events and People

Civic and Political
- Mayor was Thomas F. Mooney (1947-49).
- Population 101,310.

Commerce
- Coal exports from the docks reach a million tons a week.
- M. Mole & Son, established in Birmingham in 1835 move to Newport. They made the famous 'Mole Wrench'.
- Sir Frank Soskice Newport MP was made a Privy Councillor.
- Newport residents were congratulated for their tidiness by the council.
- Work begins on Uskmouth 'A' power station.
- HMS *Suffolk*, was scrapped at Cashmore's.

People
- First woman police officer put on traffic duty.

Places and Events
- A painting of a nude lady smoking a cigarette displayed at Town's Art Gallery caused a stir.
- Most food products still rationed but bread rationing ends .
- Lovells AFC, a Newport club, wins the Welsh Cup.
- St Peter's Church in Temple Street Pill, the Seamen's Church, closes but the Mission to Seamen at the docks reamin open. The church became the HQ for the Territorial Army and later a store. It was demolished in 1981.
- Administrative staff move from Town Hall to the Civic Centre.
- 39,000 rats killed in Newport under the Ministry of Food scheme.
- Newport Rugby team welcome the announcement that a dropped goal is to be reduced from four points to three.
- Alway school was being built.
- Newport RFC draw with Cardiff at Rodney Parade before a crowd of 24,000.
- A crowd of 20,520 watched the game between Newport County AFC and Bristol Rovers at Somerton Park.

Health
- The Royal Gwent Hospital was transferred on 5th July from Voluntary Hospital Funded status to be funded by the Government under the provision of the National Health Act 1946, and introduced by the Tredegar born Aneurin Bevan. The estimated cost of providing free treatment for each patient at the hospital was £9 4s. per year. Out-patients 4s. 11d. There was immediately a five year waiting time for some operations as previously people could not afford to have operations in hospitals. Now they were free.
- The Royal Gwent Hospital held its last fete on becoming supported by the state in 1948. £5,023 was raised.

A float called 'Soldiers of the Queen' at the 1948 Carnival. Front right was Brinley Jones (now living in Australia), the others are unknown. The hospital fete was an event that everyone looked forward to. There were dodgems, roundabouts, roll a penny stalls, coconut shys, dart throwing at playing cards etc. and even some sweet and toffee apple stalls. All of these were designed to separate you from your hard-earned cash but all in a good cause! The side shows included boxing bouts which invited you to go three rounds with 'Slogger and earn £1'!

- The National Health Service took on the financing of the hospitals and the doctors surgeries and dental service. Opticians, doctors surgeries and dentists were now free and so were well visited by those who previously could not afford to do so.

- The hospital staff also put on a pantomime or show with doctors, nurses and admin staff all playing their part. This also raised funds for keeping the Hospital going ...
- Royal Gwent Hospital at time of handover had 259 beds and St Woolos 402 beds, Allt-y-yn 57 beds, Lydia Beynon 24 beds and St Caddocs 380 beds for psychiatric patients.

1949

The British and Worldwide Scene, Events and People

- Power of the House of Lords in UK was reduced.
- Clothes rationing ends.
- Gas companies nationalised in UK in May.
- Tommy Handley, died. He was a well-known fast-talking and witty comedian and star of 'It's That Man Again' (ITMA).
- The first Scouts 'Bob-a-Job' week started in Britain.
- BBC televised its first weather forecast.
- Britain's largest ever aircraft, the 130 ton, eight-engined Bristol 'Brabazon', had its first flight. It could seat 100 passengers and had a maximum speed of 300 mph with a range of 5,500 miles. It was a commercial failure and was broken up in 1953. Its research led to the development of the larger planes in future years.
- The first comprehensive school in Britain was opened in Holyhead, Anglesey by the amalgamation of two local schools.
- Republic of Ireland proclaimed in April.
- People's Republic of China proclaimed under Chairman Mao Tse-Tung in October.
- Chinese Nationalist Government set up in Formosa in December when people fled from the mainland.
- Berlin blockade by the Russians and East Germans was lifted in May.
- Germany was divided into Federal Republic (West Germany) and the Democratic Republic (East Germany). Dr Adenauer (1876-1967) was appointed first Chancellor of West Germany in September. Professor Theodor Heus was elected the first President of East Germany.
- Twelve nations sign the North Atlantic Treaty (NATO) - stating that an attack against any one of the countries concerned would be considered to be an attack against all of them.
- The first meeting of the Council of Europe developed to create unity between the European countries in matters of human rights, democracy and social reform, etc.
- Arab-Israel armistice resulted in the partition of Jerusalem.
- South African Government adopts apartheid (separation of black and white people) as official policy.

The Local Scene, Events and People

Commerce
• Mitchell & Butler, brewers of Birmingham, buy Thatcher's Brewery in Alma Street, Pill, where until 1966 Newport citizens could take their Christmas puddings to be steamed. It was estimated that 25,000 puddings were steamed every Christmas.

People
• Evan, 4th Baronet, 2nd Viscount Tredegar, died at the age of 56 at his Surrey home. His father's brother, Frederick, became the 5th Baronet but he passed the succession of the Tredegar estate to his son John Morgan. The death of Frederick in 1954 made John the 6th Baron, Lord Tredegar.

Civic and Political
• The Mayor was Mary J. Dunn.
• Death of J.H. Thomas MP was announced.

Places and Events
• Newport County AFC get through to the 5th round of the FA Cup, beating on the way First and Second Division sides. In the 5th round they were drawn away to First Division side Portsmouth who beat the County by 3 goals to 2 after extra time.
• Newport County AFC was demoted to the Third Division.
• Holy Trinity Church, Christchurch suffers from a disastrous fire. £3,000 worth of damage. Arson suspected (5th November).
• Fire at St John the Evangelist Church Maindee. Cost of damage £45,000. Arson suspected.
• First TV signals from the newly-opened Sutton Coldfield transmitted to Newport.
• Blaen-y-Pant House at the junction of Malpas Road and Bettws Lane became the first retired persons' residence opened by the Council.
• Desmond Llewellyn became famous for his acting parts on radio and films. He was 'Q' in the James Bond films. He was born in Blaeny-pant House in 1914 where a garden was planted after his death in his memory.
• New Bus pull-in in Dock Street opened on the site of the Open Market. It became a car park when the main bus station opened.
• One way traffic in the town centre introduced.
• Clothes rationing for all clothes ends.
• Commercial Road Methodist Church celebrated its centenary.
• The Pavilion cinema and music hall, Stow Hill, closed.
• St Woolos Church given full Cathedral status.
• HMS *Ajax* scrapped at Cashmore's.

Health
• Outpatients attending Royal Gwent Hospital during the year totalled 170,739 with physiotherapy being the most attended department (56,951 attendees).

Postscript

The changes have been immense in the areas of social change, politics, industry and personal values. The period saw two major World Wars, the introduction of the uses and abuses of atomic energy, the major advances in medicine and the increase in the life expectancy due to medication and health care (when free NHS was introduced). There was a revolution in transport on land, sea and particularly air and even some thoughts of space travel (after von Braun's invention of massive rockets initially used in warfare). The geography of the world had come to the doorstep of many homes as many soldiers travelled the world to previously unthought of locations.

Education was now considered the right of the individual at the end of this period whereas it was only for the few who could afford it at the start. Secondary education was available for all and the school leaving age had risen to 15 years. The possibility of a university education was not a 'pipe dream' and finances were available for the working class children to enter higher education. The period led to mid-century optimism and the 1950s which would bring a new Queen on the throne and hopefully other changes?

Some of the materials and technology developed for warfare had benefited everyday lives including: perspex and plastics, new metallic alloys, nylon and synthetic fibres, detergents, dyes, cosmetics, clothing and a recognition of a wider range of foods from other countries. The influx of people from other nations and cultures at this time (towards the end of the 1940s) was becoming apparent. Technology was beginning to replace manpower, machines were doing what 10 men could do and the resulting concerns for the unions and bosses were becoming apparent. Men returning from World War II had different aspirations and expectations from those of 1939 and these also would have an influence on jobs, home life and society. In some homes children had no fathers during wartime but now they had and this led to some conflict. Many of the social pressures were building up and these would come to the surface and cause some heartaches in the decades to come.

We have the benefit of hindsight and can look back and see what should have been done but would it have made a difference?

References and some sources

Pillgwenlly, Newport, Cliff Knight (1983), Starling Press Ltd. ISBN 0 903434 85 7.

Pillgwenlly, Newport, Again, Cliff Knight (1984), Starling Press Ltd. ISBN 0 903434 66 0.

Pillgwenlly, Newport, The Changing Times, Cliff Knight (1985), Starling Press Ltd. ISBN 0 903434 63 6.

The New Pillgwenlly, Newport, Cliff Knight (1986), Starling Press Ltd. ISBN 0 903434 64 4.

The City of Newport, The Gateway to Wales, Terry Underwood (2005) Rompdown Ltd.

The Way We Were in Newport, Terry Underwood (1981). ISBN 0 9507908 0.

Yesterday's Newport, Terry Underwood (1980). ISBN 0 907143 00 8.

The Royal Gwent & St Woolos Hospitals - A Century of Service to Newport, compiled by Brian Peeling. Published by Old Bakehouse Publications, Abertillery. ISBN 1 874538 08 5.

Saint Julian's High School Magazine, Anniversary Brochure.

South Wales Argus Specials: 'Now and Then', Summer 1992; 'The War Years' 16th February, 1988; 'Battle of Britain Pictorial', 1980.

South Wales Echo Special, 'Yesterday' 28th March, 1989.

Photographs also supplied by Kaye Price, Bill Howell, Myra James, John Bailey and Keith Smart.